I WILL

FEAR NO EVIL

I WILL
FEAR NO EVIL

How the Lord Sustains
Us in Perilous Times

Robert L. Millet

BOOKCRAFT

SALT LAKE CITY, UTAH

Library of Congress Cataloging-in-Publication Data

Millet, Robert L.
  I will fear no evil: how the Lord sustains us in perilous times / Robert L. Millet.
    p.   cm.
  Includes bibliographical references and index.
  ISBN 1-57008-829-2 (alk. paper)
    1. Consolation. 2. Peace of mind—Religious aspects—Church of Jesus Christ of Latter-day Saints. I. Title.

BX8643.C67 2002
248.8'6—dc21   2001008083

Printed in the United States of America   54459-6959
Malloy Lithographing Incorporated, Ann Arbor, MI

10   9   8   7   6   5   4   3   2

❈ ❈

THOUGH I WALK THROUGH

THE VALLEY OF THE SHADOW

OF DEATH, I WILL FEAR NO

EVIL: FOR [GOD IS] WITH ME.

—Psalm 23:4

❈ ❈

CONTENTS

✿ ✿

PROLOGUE
THE BEST AND WORST OF TIMES

——————— ❈ ❈ ———————

What an odd day we live in! It is a day of irony, a time of sharp contrasts. At the close of the twentieth century and the last millennium, President Gordon B. Hinckley pointed out: "Now the curtains are gradually closing on this notable and exceptional century. In one respect it has been a shameful period in the history of the world. It has been the worst of all centuries, with more of war, more of man's inhumanity to man, more of conflict and trouble than any other century in the history of the world. . . .

"But in a larger sense," President Hinckley continued, "this has been the best of all centuries. In the long history of the earth there has been nothing like it. . . . This is an age of greater understanding and knowledge. . . . The miracles of modern medicine, of travel, of communication are almost beyond belief. All of this has opened new opportunities for us which we must grasp and use for the advancement of the Lord's work."[1]

And so it is on many fronts. It is the best of times and the worst of times. It is a day of great affluence, when men and women live in finer homes and enjoy more leisure moments than ever before; at the same time, more than ever before, it is a day of spreading starvation, a time when little children cry themselves to sleep amid the piercing pangs of hunger.

It is a time of information explosion, a day when we can access volumes of data in a matter of seconds; in contrast, it is a day when few of earth's inhabitants possess the discernment and sense of priority so needed in making wise and judicious decisions. Millions upon millions of people fill the ranks and pews of Christian churches today, with more persons of faith professing a belief in Jesus Christ than ever before; and yet there are greater pockets of unbelief, of professed atheism, and of creeping relativism than the planet has ever experienced.

The restored gospel, delivered to earth through the instrumentality of Joseph Smith in the nineteenth century, is spreading to all parts of the earth, and the Saints of the Most High are found on tiny islands and in booming metropolises everywhere. But our numbers remain extremely small when compared to those "who are only kept from the truth because they know not where to find it" (D&C 123:12). That is, in spite of phenomenal Church growth—for which we feel to express gratitude to our Lord—the famine for the word of God is not abated; many still "wander from sea to sea, and from the north even to the east"; they "run to and fro to seek the word of the Lord, and [do] not find it" (Amos 8:11–12).

We live in the dispensation of the fulness of times, the dispensation of dispensations; this is the final age of earth's history, in which the fulness of the gospel, including its poignant truths and its attendant powers, is on earth once again. Our dispensation represents, as it were, the ocean of divine truth into which all the revealed rivers of the past flow. The prophets or covenant spokesmen from the beginning have looked forward to and testified of our time. As the apostle

Peter taught on the day of Pentecost, this final stage of salvation history brings to pass the "restitution of all things, which God hath spoken by the mouth of all his holy prophets since the world began" (Acts 3:21). It is a terribly significant day, a day of destiny. And we have a date with destiny.

It just may be that the present generation of Saints is the most scripturally literate, the most spiritually mature, and, in general, the best prepared of any generation in history. At least that's my perspective as a religious educator for the last thirty years. When I think back on my youth and think of what we knew about the scriptures then and how often we used them in sermons and classes (we didn't know much and we didn't use them very often!), I can see clearly what a difference the new LDS editions of the scriptures and the scriptural training provided by the Church Educational System have made. That perception is juxtaposed against the stark reality that sin and vice and perversion now make their way into our homes and our personal lives more readily than ever before. While the knowledge and power of our Savior is now penetrating every continent and visiting every clime and country, the diabolical teachings of the "god of this world" are broadcast on television, in the movies, in magazines, and through the internet.

In short, this is a day that easily confuses and confounds most of earth's inhabitants. It is, in fact, a singular time, an unusual era that will require singular and unusual souls to engage the contradictions and bring order out of spreading chaos. That's the task before us, a daunting task to be sure. But I believe we're up to it. With divine assistance, we can handle it. We need not fret or fear, for truly "they that be with us are more than they that be with them" (2 Kings 6:16). Our God is our ally, and he will stand by us as we face what would otherwise be insurmountable odds. We are not here by chance but rather by design, as a part of a grand plan of salvation. We are not novices in regard to either championing eternal things or confronting organized evil. Rather, we are seasoned veterans, for we already have under our belt the experience (though veiled from conscious memory) of standing valiantly on the side of Elohim and Jehovah and opposing the forces of Lucifer in a distant past. John the Revelator thus noted that the faithful in the first estate overcame the father of all lies "by the blood of the Lamb, and by the word of their testimony" (Revelation 12:11).

In speaking to the saintly Job, the Lord Jehovah asked this penetrating question: "Where wast thou when I laid the foundations of the earth? declare, if thou hast understanding. . . . When the morning stars sang together, and all the sons of God shouted for joy?" (Job 38:4, 7). Many of us, having passed through personal or family turmoil, or having witnessed unspeakable tragedy in our time, might be prone (in our weaker moments) to ask: What was all the shouting about? Knowing what we know, we inquire: What were the sons and daughters of God so excited about? Why were they so eager to come to earth, especially when they may well have been aware of the pain and frustration and heartache and irony associated with this life?

Once again, despite the odds, despite the strength and sophistication of evil and the prevailing trauma in mortality, we can make it to the end of the road of life, and we can do so with quiet confidence and assurance. "Who are you?" President Harold B. Lee once asked the Saints. "You are all the sons and daughters of God. Your spirits were created and lived as organized intelligences before the world was. You have been blessed to have a physical body because of your obedience to certain commandments in that premortal state. You are now born into a family to which you have come, into the nations through which you have come, as a reward for the kind of lives you lived before you came here and at a time in the world's history . . . determined by the faithfulness of each of those who lived before this world was created."[2]

Such understanding can fortify us against surrendering to the devil or resigning ourselves to defeat at the hands of a cruel and seemingly unfair world. "Now, my brethren and sisters," President Hinckley implored, "the time has come for us to stand a little taller, to lift our eyes and stretch our minds to a greater comprehension and understanding of the grand millennial mission of this, The Church of Jesus Christ of Latter-day Saints. This is a season to be strong. It is a time to move forward without hesitation, knowing well the meaning, the breadth, and the importance of our mission. . . .

"We have nothing to fear. God is at the helm. He will overrule for the good of this work. He will shower down blessings upon those who walk in obedience to His commandments. Such has been His promise. Of His ability to keep that promise none of us can doubt."[3]

Most of us can deal with any *how* if we simply know *why*. We are able to move on, to move ahead, through gaining perspective, through coming to see things, at least to some degree, as God does. That's what this book is all about. It's about finding light in a darkening world; leaning upon certainty when so many things are uncertain; becoming more sensitive to evil without being obsessed about it; acting responsibly in a society that refuses to take responsibility; discovering reservoirs of faith and courage at those times when we feel so very weak and alone and helpless; and living happily and peacefully in the midst of prolonged misery.

NOTES

    1. Conference Report, April 1999, 116.

    2. Conference Report, October 1973, 7.

    3. Conference Report, April 1995, 95.

I

GOD AND HUMAN TRAGEDY

As I sit at my computer and write these words, it occurs to me that it has been only a short time since terrorists hijacked three commercial airliners and flew the planes (with their passengers) into the twin towers of the World Trade Center in New York City and the Pentagon in Washington, D.C. A fourth plane was kept from the hijackers' nefarious purposes only by the heroism of persons on board. Thousands of innocent victims died from these horrid acts. It is impossible to fathom the depth of human emotion, to comprehend the anguish and heartache—as well as the suspicion, anxiety, and fear—that have come as a result of these tragedies. In many ways, no matter where we live, our lives will never be the same again.

Life is good, and, to be sure, there are moments and seasons in life that make it all worthwhile, that whisper peace and assurance to our souls, that affirm that "men are, that they might have joy" (2 Nephi 2:25). But there are times when our sense of wellness is shaken to the core, occasions when we bow our heads, weep, and cry out, as did the Prophet Joseph Smith, "O God, where art thou?" (D&C 121:1). Indeed, when we think of the nightmare of the Holocaust, as well as the devilish and unnecessary loss of life under countless totalitarian regimes, we find ourselves saying, "Wait a minute! This isn't the way things are supposed to be!"

One evangelical scholar, Cornelius Plantinga, has observed: "In the film *Grand Canyon*, an immigration attorney breaks out of a traffic jam and attempts to bypass it. His route takes him along streets that seem progressively darker and more deserted. Then the predictable . . . nightmare: his expensive car stalls on one of those alarming streets whose teenage guardians favor expensive guns and sneakers. The attorney does manage to phone for a tow truck, but before it arrives, five young street toughs surround his disabled car and threaten him with considerable bodily harm. Then, just in time, the tow truck shows up and its driver—an earnest, genial man—begins to hook up to the disabled car. The toughs protest: the truck driver is interrupting their meal. So the driver takes the leader of the group aside and attempts a five-sentence introduction to metaphysics: 'Man,' he says, 'the world ain't supposed to work like this. Maybe you don't know that, but this ain't the way it's supposed to be. I'm supposed to be able to do my job without askin' you if I can. And that dude is supposed to be able to wait with his car without you rippin' him off. Everything's supposed to be different than what it is here.'"[1]

No, things aren't the way they ought to be. And they haven't been since Adam and Eve left the Garden of Eden. This is a fallen world, a telestial tenement, and we are brought face to face on a regular basis with the fact that for this temporal time and season not all well-laid plans will come to fruition. Times change. Youth fades. Things break down. Bodies grow old and decay. I look at the date and realize that only three months ago today I was rushed to the hospital after suffering a serious heart attack. I walk a little slower now, don't have the stamina I once had, and in general feel like the old tabernacle is gradually losing the battle against mortality.

Because there is pain, because there is sorrow, because there is tragedy, men and women ask: Where is God, especially when it hurts? In speaking to Brigham Young University students many years ago, Elder Spencer W. Kimball asked some tough questions about human suffering and tragedy, and at the same time provided a provocative and elevated perspective on God:

"Was it the Lord who directed the plane into the mountain to snuff out the lives of its occupants, or were there mechanical faults or human errors?

"Did our Father in heaven cause the collision of the cars that took six people into eternity, or was it the error of the driver who ignored safety rules?

"Did God take the life of the young mother or prompt the child to toddle into the canal or guide the other child into the path of the oncoming car?

"Did the Lord cause the man to suffer a heart attack? Was the death of the missionary untimely? Answer, if you can. I cannot, for though I know God has a major role in our lives, I do not know how much he causes to happen and how much he merely permits. . . .

"Could the Lord have prevented these tragedies? The answer is, Yes. The Lord is omnipotent, with all power to control our lives, save us pain, prevent all accidents, drive all planes and cars, feed us, protect us, save us from labor, effort, sickness, even from death, if he will. But he will not. . . .

"The basic gospel law is free agency and eternal development. To force us to be careful or righteous would be to nullify that fundamental law and make growth impossible."[2]

Following the deaths of the apostles in the meridian of time, and the consequent loss of divine authority and plain and precious scriptural truths, men and women groped in darkness. Within four centuries after Christ's ascension, church councils were convened to settle the matter of the nature of God and the Godhead. In an effort to reconcile Christian theology with Greek philosophy, the god of Nicea and Chalcedon and Constantinople was created: a being without body and parts; a being who is timeless, immutable (unchangeable), and impassible (incapable of feeling or emotion). The god of the philosophers was the unknowable one, the untouchable one, the unreachable one. Further, over time and in a misguided effort to confess and acknowledge God's total sovereignty, theologians devised the notion of deity's complete control over all things, including men's and women's actions.

It is especially challenging for persons who view God solely as a dispenser of good gifts and happy times to fathom how and in what manner he is related, if at all, to earthly trauma. Having been brought up on a constant diet of "God is love" or "God is good," they inevitably equate such goodness with kindness. "By the goodness of God," C. S. Lewis pointed out, "we mean nowadays almost exclusively His lovingness; and in this we may be right. And by Love, in this context, most of us mean kindness—the desire to see others than the self happy; not happy in this way or in that, but just happy. What would really satisfy us would be a God who said of anything we happened to like doing, 'What does it matter so long as they are contented?' We want, in fact, not so much a Father in Heaven as a grandfather in heaven—a senile benevolence who, as they say, 'liked to see young people enjoying themselves,' and whose plan for the universe was simply that it might be truly said at the end of each day, 'a good time was had by all.'"[3]

Through the instrumentality of a modern prophet, light and truth and understanding concerning the true nature of God have come to us. The God we have come to know is an exalted Man, a Man of Holiness (Moses 6:57), a divine being who has all power and all knowledge and who possesses every godly attribute in perfection. At the same time, through the clarifying lenses provided by the revelations of the Restoration, the Latter-day Saints are made acquainted with a God who is in reality our Heavenly Father, the Father of our spirits; who "has a body of flesh and bones as tangible as man's" (D&C 130:22); who feels tender regard for all his children and is, like his Beloved Son, "touched with the feeling of our infirmities" (Hebrews 4:15); and who has granted to each of us moral agency, the capacity to choose what we will do with our lives. As Elder Kimball pointed out in the statement above, agency is paramount. In fact, as we know, agency was one of the central issues in the war in heaven (Moses 4:3)—a war, by the way, that is still under way. We also know, in a very personal way, of the reality of evil and of the fact that Lucifer is bent upon our destruction and the overthrow of the Father's plan. He does everything in his power to pervert and corrupt the right way and to entice men and women to use their agency unwisely.

There are some things that are even more horrible to contemplate than the Holocaust, more unspeakable than millions of innocent people being put to death by crazed dictators, more frightening than terrorists hijacking planes and murdering thousands. Consider this thought: What if there were no agency? What if people did not have the right to choose?

What if Lucifer's amendatory proposals in the grand councils of heaven had been implemented?

We rejoice to know that agency is an eternal reality, one of the greatest of all the gifts of a benevolent and generous God. But, of course, that gift comes at a price. The power to choose automatically brings with it the possibility of improper, unwise, immoral, and evil choices and thus abuse and human tragedy.

One philosopher wrote: "A God who gives humans such free will necessarily brings about the possibility, and puts outside his own control whether or not . . . evil occurs. It is not logically possible—that is, it would be self-contradictory to suppose—that God could give us such free will and yet ensure that we always use it in the right way. . . .

". . . A world in which agents can benefit each other but not do each other harm is one where they have only very limited responsibility for each other. If my responsibility for you is limited to whether or not to give you a camcorder, but I cannot cause you pain, stunt your growth, or limit your education, then I do not have a great deal of responsibility for you. . . . A good God, like a good father, will delegate responsibility. In order to allow creatures a share in creation, he will allow them the choice of hurting and maiming, of frustrating the divine plan."

Now note these perceptive insights: "I am fortunate if the natural possibility of my suffering if you choose to hurt me is the vehicle which makes your choice really matter. My vulnerability, my openness to suffering (which necessarily involves my actually suffering if you make the wrong choice), means that you are not just like a pilot in a simulator, where it does not matter if mistakes are made. That our choices matter tremendously, that we can make great differences to things for good or ill, is one of the greatest gifts a creator can give us. And if my suffering is the means by which he can give you that choice, I too am in this respect fortunate."[4]

Where is God when it hurts? He is in his heavens. He is aware. He knows. In ways that we cannot even comprehend, he knows. And he blesses and lifts and liberates and lightens the burdens of his children whenever he can. But he cannot remove us from the toils and tragedies and contradictions of life—whether they come from agency or simply from the challenges of this existence—without robbing us of mortal experience. These things come with the turf. They are part of the test. So much depends upon how we choose to think about what most consider to be the unfairness and the senseless nature of temporal trauma. So much depends upon what we understand about God our Father, about his plan of salvation, and about how vital it is for us to move ahead, even when our burdens or the burdens of others seem unbearable.

While a measure of joy and happiness and a sense of overcoming can be ours in this life, the fulness of joy is reserved for the next estate, when spirit and body are reunited in the resurrection (D&C 93:33). "Wherefore, fear not even unto death," the Redeemer declared, "for in this world your joy is not full, but in me your joy is full" (D&C 101:36). Or, as President Boyd K. Packer explained, "There are three parts to the plan. You are in the second or the middle part, the one in which you will be tested by temptation, by trials, perhaps by tragedy. Understand that, and you will be better able to make sense of life and to resist the disease of doubt and despair and depression. . . .

"If you expect to find only ease and peace and bliss during

Act II, you surely will be frustrated. You will understand little of what is going on and why it is permitted to be as [it is].

"Remember this! The line 'And they all lived happily ever after' is never written into the second act. That line belongs in the third act when the mysteries are solved and everything is put right."[5]

As Elder Neal A. Maxwell taught, "When we tear ourselves free from the entanglements of the world, are we promised a religion of repose or an Eden of ease? No! We are promised tears and trials and toil! But we are also promised final triumph, the mere contemplation of which tingles one's soul."[6]

We shouted for joy in that premortal day (Job 38:7) because we knew that there were lasting lessons and everlasting principles to be learned on earth, things we could neither grasp nor experience in our first estate. We shouted for joy because we knew that there were relationships to be developed, feelings to be felt, tests to be passed. And we shouted for joy—knowing full well the struggle through which we would be called upon to pass—because we knew that it would be worth it.

NOTES

1. *Not the Way It's Supposed to Be*, 7.

2. *Faith Precedes the Miracle*, 96.

3. *The Problem of Pain*, 35–36.

4. Richard Swinburne, *Is There a God?* 98–103.

5. "The Play and the Plan," CES Fireside, 7 May 1995, 2–3; emphasis removed.

6. Conference Report, October 1974, 16.

2

VIGILANCE WITHOUT FEAR

I t is extremely difficult to pass through a crisis, learn the appropriate lessons, be adequately forewarned, and move on with life without at the same time becoming over-sensitive and hyperalert to possible future recurrences. Because my wife and I have had some experience with wandering children, I can say without hesitation that siblings younger than the wanderer are in for a rough time! Why? Because Mom and Dad have been through the perilous times once and have no desire to see such tragedies reenacted in the lives of their younger children. The temptation to the parents is to be unusually (and often unnecessarily) suspicious, leery, much more strict and regimented, and prone to react quickly to the slightest aberration from the family standard.

Men or women who have been "burned" in dating or courtship may be prone to "hunker down" and refuse to allow themselves to meet new people or even approximate close and endearing relationships in the future. Those who have gone through a tempestuous marriage characterized by constant disharmony will be much less open to the sharing of their true feelings and much more inclined to "hold back" a bit, sensing that they must never again wear their feelings on their sleeve.

And so it goes through most of life's experiences: we want to learn from the pain and avoid it at all costs in the future.

But life is meant to be lived. We cannot allow ourselves to be stifled and stilted by events of the past, no matter how traumatic or life-changing they were. I was assigned many years ago to work with two men who had been quarreling for a decade. After meeting with both of them, I learned that Persons A and B had at one time been best friends. They had grown up together, double-dated, married young women who were also friends, and lived not far from one another for the first several years of their married lives. One day Person A confided something to Person B. It was not a big thing, just a private matter that Person A asked B to keep to himself. In a moment of weakness some months later, Person B mentioned the confidential matter in a rather public setting, the word got back to A, and the caustic accusations began. "I will never trust you again with anything," he said to his friend. "Nor will I ever forgive you for what you have done."

Person A was true to his word. Despite my pleadings for a reconciliation and the additional efforts of a score of priesthood leaders and friends over many, many years, Person A refused to let the matter drop and forgive. To my knowledge, he has maintained bitterness bordering on hatred for about thirty years now. I have watched with much interest and deep sorrow as this incident—almost silly, given how relatively unimportant the matter was—has cankered the soul of Person A, driven him deeper into his own hostilities and away from people, and eaten away at his spirituality and overall zest for life. And in some ways, even more tragically, it is as though Person B is being held hostage by Person A, unable to receive forgiveness, to move on, to find peace. He too has been beaten down by one foolish man's refusal to let go and bounce back.

Life is too short for us to be held hostage by our own past, the deeds of others we know and love (even cruel and unkind ones), or even the evil inflicted by insidious strangers bent on our destruction. One family I know experienced a break-in and robbery in their home while they were away one weekend. The mother indicated that she and the children felt somehow defiled, that their privacy and sacred space had been violated. The family began to plan ahead to forestall any and all efforts to disturb their peace in the future. They added to their security system a large number of locks, several alarms, and dogs in the house and in the yard to announce intruders. In addition, the father of the family began to build quite an arsenal of weapons. Family members gradually began to leave home less and less often and, when they did, they left two or more members at the house to stand guard. Truly, this family had allowed an unfortunate event, a painful one to be sure, to transform them from a happy, easygoing brood to a little army possessed of a siege mentality.

As I mentioned earlier, the United States as a nation has recently been bludgeoned and jolted by unfeeling persons who viciously hijacked passenger planes and killed thousands of innocent people. While appropriate security measures, requiring some degree of inconvenience on the part of the average citizen, can and should be taken to lessen the risk of future terrorist attacks of this sort, life must go on. For Americans or any other people in the free world to allow themselves to be frightened into the shadows is to concede a victory to the perpetrators of this heinous deed. Rather, we will go about our business and have no hesitation about air travel. That is, while we will be vigilant—on our guard, prepared—we will refuse to live in fear. Nor will we be controlled by fear. "The fear of man bringeth a snare: but whoso putteth his trust in the Lord shall be safe" (Proverbs 29:25).

The wisest among us also refuse to allow fear to set our agenda. One of the leaders of the Church once related to a group of us that not long after he had been called as a General Authority someone planted a bomb at the door of the Salt Lake Temple. The bomb had exploded and knocked the large, heavy door off its hinges. He commented that the episode was chilling to him and created an anxiety and discomfort, a fear, that lasted all day. To his utter surprise, he noticed that all through the day, in the many meetings he attended with other General Authorities, no mention was made of this scary incident. Finally, at the end of the day, he asked one of the senior Brethren about the temple door, only to have his colleague remark, "Yes, we need to get that fixed, don't we." Then he added this important principle, one that ought to guide our walk and talk as we move into troublesome days ahead: "We do not take counsel from our fears."

Truly, as we sing in the hymn,

> *I will not doubt, I will not fear;*
> *God's love and strength are always near.*
> *His promised gift helps me to find*
> *An inner strength and peace of mind.*
> *I give the Father willingly*
> *My trust, my prayers, humility.*
> *His Spirit guides; his love assures*
> *That fear departs when faith endures.*[1]

President Gordon B. Hinckley has asked the question: "Who among us can say that he or she has not felt fear? . . . We suffer from the fear of ridicule, the fear of failure, the fear of loneliness, the fear of ignorance. Some fear the present, some the future. . . . Let us recognize that fear comes not of God, but rather that this gnawing, destructive element comes from the adversary of truth and righteousness. Fear is the antithesis of faith. It is corrosive in its effects, even deadly.

" 'For God hath not given us the spirit of fear; but of power, and of love, and of a sound mind.' (2 Timothy 1:7.)

"These principles are the great antidotes to the fears that rob us of our strength and sometimes knock us down to defeat. They give us power.

"What power? The power of the gospel, the power of truth, the power of faith, the power of the priesthood."[2]

Although it is well to be in a vigilant position militarily or socially or economically, perhaps the greatest antidote to fear is closeness to the Lord, an eagerness on our part to cultivate his Spirit and seek to obtain his power and strength. We have been instructed that "if ye are prepared ye shall not fear" (D&C 38:30). Perfect love, the pure love of Christ, casts out fear (1 John 4:18; Moroni 8:16). As members of the Lord's Church, having the gift of the Holy Ghost, we are entitled to a rich outpouring of his peace, an endowment that will dispel fear. "If this generation harden not their hearts," the Savior declared in a modern revelation, "I will establish my church among them. . . . Therefore, whosoever belongeth to my church need not fear, for such shall inherit the kingdom of heaven" (D&C 10:53, 55). Again, note the promise to his Saints: "Wherefore, be of good cheer, and do not fear, for I the Lord am with you, and will stand by you" (D&C 68:6).

Notes

1. Naomi W. Randall, "When Faith Endures," in *Hymns of The Church of Jesus Christ of Latter-day Saints*, no. 128.

2. *Teachings of Gordon B. Hinckley*, 220–21.

3

AMBIGUITY AND UNCERTAINTY

There's a very real sense in which we as Latter-day Saints—and recipients of a myriad of restored truths—are spoiled! We have the answers to so many questions, the solutions to so many of the world's vexing issues, the only meaningful suggestion for peace in a troubled world, peace here and hereafter. In fact, we have so many answers to so many religious questions that some of us expect to have them all. And it's downright unsettling when we happen upon some dilemma or face some tragedy for which no answer or rational explanation is forthcoming, something which is at best unclear or at worst unrevealed.

It is the nature of mankind to seek for closure, to strive to fill in the blanks. That is as it should be. Our souls reach out for answers. We are eternal creatures living in a mortal world, spiritual beings undergoing a temporal experience. The veil of forgetfulness purposely and purposefully denies us access to many things we once knew, many parts of a rather intricate and complex puzzle. Even with all that has been delivered by prophets and apostles, by wise men and women, and by the spirit of inspiration, there are and will be questions. Difficult questions. Startling developments. Nagging issues that are troublesome and at times seemingly unanswerable.

It is important to note that there is no evil in having questions, no harm in wondering and asking and inquiring. No person, Latter-day Saint or otherwise, ought to feel guilty because
he or she has questions. Such is perfectly normal, a part of the
plan. If we already possessed the solutions to all the traumas
and the formulas for all the paradoxes, there would be little
purpose and certainly little fulfillment to be had in this second
estate. Success and happiness in life depend not on whether
we have questions but rather with how we deal with them.
Whatever the nature of our queries, there are both productive
and counterproductive, both fruitful and unfruitful means of
engaging them.

Some years ago my family and I moved from a part of the
country we had come to love dearly. I was asked to assume a
new assignment in the Church Educational System that
required a relocation. We had been in our new home for only a
few weeks when I received a telephone call late one Sunday
evening. The woman on the other end of the line was deeply
distraught. "Brother Millet," she said, "this is Sister Johnson."

"Yes, Sister Johnson," I responded. "How are you and the
family?" I had known the Johnson family quite well; they lived
in the area we had just left. Brother Johnson had been a member of the bishopric in their ward (Sister Johnson had served
in the presidencies of both the Primary and Relief Society)
while I had served as a member of the stake presidency in that
area. I had been in their home several times, had enjoyed din-
ners and social gatherings with them, had known of their dedi-
cated Church service, and believed them to be one of the most
settled and secure Latter-day Saint families anywhere. They
had joined the Church after having been found and taught by
the missionaries some ten years earlier. They were themselves

extremely missionary-minded and had been instrumental in leading several families to baptism. But there was obvious pain in Sister Johnson's voice. I tried to be positive and asked: "What can I do for you?"

"I desperately need your help," she said. "My husband is about to leave the Church."

Her statement nearly took my breath. "Leave the Church?" I asked. "What do you mean?"

She went on to explain that her husband's brother, a man not of our faith who had opposed their baptism, had for several months been sending rather bitter anti-Mormon propaganda through the mail. She mentioned that at first her husband had ignored the stuff, but that after a few weeks he began perusing it out of sheer curiosity. "I began to notice a gradual change in Bill," she stated. She pointed out that he became argumentative and uncooperative at Church, touchy and ill at ease at home, and just plain unsettled in his demeanor. "He has a lot of questions, Brother Millet," she added, "and I'm afraid if he doesn't get them answered pretty soon we'll lose him."

"How can I help?" I inquired.

"He wants to talk with you," Sister Johnson came back.

"Good," I said. "Put him on the line."

"Oh no," she said, "he wants to meet with you in person."

I expressed to her that such a meeting would be perfectly fine with me, but that we were now some ten or twelve hours' driving distance from one another. I suggested that if this was the only way to deal with his concerns, if his concerns could not be addressed by someone in their area, then we should set a time when we might get together.

"He's already on his way," she then observed. "He left a

couple of hours ago. Would you please meet with him? He'll be at the institute by 9:00 A.M."

I was a bit startled but quickly assured Sister Johnson that I would be more than happy to meet with him and do what I could.

Brother Johnson wasn't the only one who didn't sleep that night. I tossed and turned through the night, arose several times, and retired to the living room to pray for guidance. The morning came faster than I had wished, and my stomach churned as I contemplated what the meeting might entail. Sister Johnson was quite accurate in her prediction: her husband arrived a little after nine o'clock. She was also quite accurate in her description of her husband's condition. He had a fallen countenance, a dark look in his eyes, and in general a rather gloomy appearance; this simply was not the man I had known before. He had lost the Spirit and was in many ways like a broken man, like a person who had lost his innocence, who indeed had lost his way. We knelt and prayed together, and I pleaded with the Lord to dispel the spirit of gloom and doubt and endow us with the spirit of light and understanding. The answer to that prayer came eventually, but only after a long and difficult struggle.

As is so often the case, Brother Johnson had been confronted with scores of questions on authority, on the Church's claim to being Christian, on temple rites, on doctrinal teachings of specific Church leaders, on changes in scripture or Church practice, and so forth and so on. An endless list. I took the time to respond to every issue, to suggest an answer if such was possible. In some cases the answer was simply a call for faith, an invitation to pray or repray about whether Joseph Smith was a prophet of God, whether his successors have worn the same mantle of authority, and whether the Church is divinely led today. I sensed, however, that there was something deeper, something beneath the surface that was being reflected in his questions, something that was festering and eating away at his soul like a cancer. It took me almost eight hours to discover what that something was.

When Brother and Sister Johnson were first taught the gospel and introduced to the Book of Mormon, one of the missionaries—no doubt well-meaning but shortsighted—had said something like this: "Now, Brother and Sister Johnson, the Book of Mormon is true. It came from God to Joseph Smith. And you can know for yourselves that it is true by praying about it. But, the fact is, there are so many archaeological evidences of its truthfulness, these days it almost isn't necessary to pray about it!" The statement sounded convincing enough. Brother Johnson bought into that line of reasoning and—shortsighted on his own part—never took occasion to pray with real intent about the Book of Mormon. When anti-Mormon materials suggested that there were not as many current external evidences of the Nephite or Jaredite civilizations as he had been told previously, his whole world collapsed. If the Book of Mormon wasn't true, he reasoned, then Joseph Smith was not a prophet. If Joseph Smith was not a prophet . . . And so on. One fatal step led to another. And now he was ready to throw it all away, unfortunately because his testimony was not substantive, his doctrinal foundation weak and shifting. And he had been unwilling to exercise sufficient faith and patience to resee and refocus on the things that really count, in this case the message or content of the Book of Mormon.

It was almost a relief to finally get down to the core issue. I explained to him that we were now up against the wall of faith and that the only issue to be decided was whether or not he was willing to pay the price to know the truth. I asked some hard questions, such as: Did you ever know that this work is true? What was your witness based on? What has this doubting and this vexation of the soul done to your wife and children? Does the bitter spirit you have felt during the last few months come from God? And then I asked: Are you willing to throw it all away, to jettison all that is good and ennobling because your foundation was deficient? He paused, reflected again with me on the painful and poignant strugglings he had undergone, but then added that he wanted more than anything to feel once more what he had felt ten years earlier. I stressed to him the need to stay with simple and solid doctrinal matters, particularly in regard to the Book of Mormon and the Restoration, to focus on the things of greatest worth, to follow the same course of study and pondering and prayer that he had followed during his initial investigation of the Church. I challenged him never to yield to the temptation to quit the Church when he encountered things he didn't understand, especially when there were so many things he *did* understand and know. It was a sweet experience to watch the light of faith and trust come back into his countenance and into his life.

This experience highlights the tragic reality that too often people are prone to "jump ship," to forsake family and friends and faith—to give it all up—because there is an unanswered question, an unresolved dilemma, or a new development in life that defies explanation. Let me briefly share a different experience. Several years ago I became acquainted with a lovely young family who joined the Church—a mother, father, and two children. From all appearances they were a perfect conversion: people who loved the Church, eager to jump in with both feet, and anxious to share their newfound way of life with others. Sister Brown was quickly absorbed into the Primary, while Brother Brown became fast friends with members of the elders quorum. After they had been in the Church for well over a year, Brother Brown came to see me at my office one day. He expressed his love for the Church as well as the thrill he felt at seeing his family deeply rooted in Mormonism. But he then shared with me something that I never would have supposed—he did not really have a witness of Joseph Smith's prophetic calling. He said, in essence: "Bob, I love the gospel with all my heart. I know that this is the true Church. There's no question in my mind about it. This is what I want for my family, now and always. But I have a problem, one that won't seem to go away. I just don't know that Joseph Smith was a prophet."

He then expressed how silly such a thing must sound to me, that is, to accept and embrace the revelation and at the same time be unable to accept and acknowledge the revelator. He said, "I've prayed and prayed and prayed for a testimony of Joseph Smith, but I still can't say that I know he was called of God. I sincerely believe that he was a great and good man and that in the purest sense he was inspired of God. But I just don't know for sure that he was a prophet. What do I do?" This was a bit unusual to me. From all I could discern, there was no duplicity, no cynicism, no skepticism, only simple and pure uncertainty; he wanted so badly to know, but he didn't know. We worked together on this problem for years. We read books on Joseph Smith; we fasted together; we prayed together. In all that time, Brother Brown remained true and faithful. He labored in many of the auxiliaries of the Church and for a time served as an elders quorum president. He and his family were active and involved in every way that could be expected of them. Our families became quite close, and we often spent time talking about life and its challenges, about the central place of the gospel in our lives, and about where we would be if we were not members of the Church.

In time we moved from the area. It was several years later that I received a telephone call from Brother Brown. "Bob," he said excitedly, "I have something to tell you. I have a testimony of Joseph Smith. These feelings have been growing within me for several months now, but I can finally stand and say that I know. I know!" I wept with him as we talked about the peace of mind he had gained, as we discussed this most recent phase of his lengthy but steady conversion. It had taken almost a decade for him to come to know, but in the interim he had done all that was expected of him.

I have a witness of how much the Lord loves Brother Brown and all the other Brother Browns who have the spiritual stamina and moral courage to hang on, to hold to the rod, even when they are not absolutely certain as to the destination of the path they traverse or what they will do in a brand-new life situation. Surely this is what the Savior meant when he counseled us: "Search diligently, pray always, and be believing, and all things shall work together for your good, if ye walk uprightly and remember the covenant wherewith ye have covenanted one with another" (D&C 90:24).

Another example of a counterproductive approach to obtaining answers is going to the wrong people for help. A man and his wife that I knew quite well joined the Church in the southern part of the United States. After a year's involvement with the Church, they traveled to Washington, D.C., to receive the blessings of the temple. On returning home, the father had several unanswered questions about the temple, so he contacted his former Protestant minister and arranged for a meeting. The minister, of course, was more than willing to oblige him and especially eager to give answers to his queries regarding Mormon temples. As one might suppose, the family left the Church within a matter of weeks and returned to their former religion. Simply stated, one would not go to Caiaphas or Pilate to learn about Jesus. He would go to Peter, James, or John, those who knew the Master intimately. One does not go to the enemies of Joseph Smith or the critics of the present Church if he or she sincerely wants to gain understanding concerning the faith. Wisdom would suggest that one does not take his doubts to a known doubter and expect to receive peace of mind.

Each of us is under obligation to search and ponder the issues ourselves, to do our best to learn by study and by faith the answers to our concerns (D&C 9:7–9; 88:118). Every member of this Church has a direct channel to our Heavenly Father; there is no one between us and God. Every person who has been baptized and confirmed has a right to the companionship and guidance of the Holy Ghost, the Comforter, even that Spirit of Truth which knows all things (D&C 42:17; Moses 6:61). In addition, members of a given ward can readily take their concerns to their priesthood leaders—their branch president or bishop. If the bishop does not know the answer to the question, he can inquire of the stake president. If the stake president is unable to address the concern and feels it advisable to do so, he may inquire of the General Authorities of the Church. As indicated earlier, people ought to feel free to ask their questions. If an answer is to be had, it can be obtained through proper channels. There is a temptation, when we are troubled by a particular matter, to spend inordinate amounts of time researching it. Some things simply have not been revealed, and thus to devote ourselves endlessly to the discovery of what in essence is the undiscoverable (at least for now) is counterproductive. It's almost a waste of time, especially when our efforts could so much more profitably be expended in studying and reinforcing the things that *have* been given by God.

We reduce the realm of the unknown not by wandering in it but rather by delighting in and expanding our knowledge of that which God has already revealed. It is a soul-satisfying experience to be reading Topic A and then to have our minds caught away to consider Topic B. Indeed, serious, consistent, prayerful consideration and reflection upon the *institutional* revelations (the standard works and the words of the living oracles) result in *individual* revelations, including—where the Lord senses it is appropriate and we are ready to receive them—the answers to our more difficult questions. Those answers may come as a specific response to a specific concern, or they may come in the form of a comforting and peaceful assurance that all is well, that God is in his heaven, that the work in which we are engaged is true, that specifics will be made known in the Lord's due time. Either way, answers do come. They really do, but only as we go to the right source.

Some people jump to the false and really rather silly conclusion that because they do not understand, then no one else does either. That's quite a presumptuous conclusion, but it is, nevertheless, a surprisingly common one. Humility would demand a different stance. Meekness would force us to acknowledge that there just might be someone either brighter or more experienced than ourselves, or maybe even someone who has successfully struggled with this issue before. Common sense would suggest that the odds are against absolute originality in regard to our specific concern. And even if it is possible that we have indeed unearthed something which no other mortal has ever encountered, still there are good and wise people in our midst who have been blessed with the gifts of the Spirit—with discernment, with revelation, with wisdom and judgment—to assist us in putting all things into proper perspective.

A related tendency with some is to parade their doubts, to suppose that by making a public announcement of all things that trouble them they shall somehow either feel better about their difficulties or identify and join hands with others who similarly struggle. Of course, as we have suggested already, one is not expected to suffer alone. There is help available, within fairly easy reach. Precious little good comes, however, from "hanging out our dirty wash," from making public proclamations about one's inner anxieties, little good to the individual and little good to groups of people. Such things merely feed doubt and perpetuate it. "Why are a few members," asked Elder Neal A. Maxwell, "who somewhat resemble the ancient Athenians, so eager to hear some new doubt or criticism? (see Acts 17:21). Just as some weak members slip across a state line to gamble, a few go out of their way to have their doubts titillated. Instead of nourishing their faith, they are gambling 'off-shore' with their fragile faith. To the question 'Will ye also go away?' these few would reply, 'Oh, no, we merely want a weekend pass in order to go to a casino for critics or a clubhouse for cloakholders.' Such easily diverted members are not disciples but fair-weather followers.

"Instead," Elder Maxwell concluded, "true disciples are

rightly described as steadfast and immovable, pressing forward with 'a perfect brightness of hope' (2 Nephi 31:20; see also D&C 49:23)."[1]

With some questions we may simply be able to ask ourselves: "Does this really matter? Is this issue important enough to worry myself about? Is it worth the effort?" We have only so much time and energy in this life; we would do well to ignore, where possible, the unimportant, to avoid getting caught up, as someone has suggested, in the thick of thin things! As a professor of religion at Brigham Young University, I have found it fascinating (and sometimes a bit discouraging) to find what some students grapple with. This one just has to know the exact location of Kolob. That one won't rest until he has calculated the precise dimensions of the celestial city seen by John the Revelator. Others wrestle with the present resting place of the Ark of the Covenant or Joseph Smith's seer stone. "There is so much to learn about the great eternal verities which shape our destiny," Elder Bruce R. McConkie has written, "that it seems a shame to turn our attention everlastingly to the minutiae and insignificant things. So often questions like this are asked: 'I know it is not essential to my salvation, but I would really like to know how many angels can dance on the head of a pin and if it makes any difference whether the pin is made of brass or bronze?' There is such a thing as getting so tied up with little fly specks on the great canvas which depicts the whole plan of salvation that we lose sight of what the life and the light and the glory of eternal reward are all about. (See, e.g., Matt. 23:23–25.) There is such a thing as virtually useless knowledge, the acquisition of which won't make one iota of difference to the destiny of the kingdom or the salvation of its subjects."[2]

In teaching some of my religion classes, I have occasionally said that it is as important to know *what we do not know* as it is to know what we know. Further, to quarrel and dispute over the unknown and the unrevealed is fruitless and absolutely unnecessary. In that spirit, it is fundamentally necessary for us occasionally to say, "I don't know!" Part of our spiritual maturity is reflected in our ability to deal with ambiguity, to handle uncertainty. And yet our focus need not be upon the unknown; rather, we can emphasize what we *do* know. This is the pattern found in scripture, the pattern whereby a prophet says, in essence, "I don't know this, but let me tell you what I do know." An angel asked Nephi: "Knowest thou the condescension of God?" Now note the young prophet's response: "I know that he loveth his children; nevertheless, I do not know the meaning of all things" (1 Nephi 11:16–17; compare Alma 7:8; 40:8–9).

There are many things we will need to wait on, many questions we will encounter whose answers will definitely not be forthcoming right away. Some things we need to be willing to "put on a shelf." We continue our searching, our prayer, our discussions, but we wait patiently upon the Lord. I, like many others, do not understand for the present all the things that took place in the history of our Church or all the doctrines preached by leaders of the Church. But my confidence and my trust in Joseph Smith and his successors is implicit. We simply do not have the whole story yet. We must be patient, avoiding the temptation to attribute improper motivation or to jump prematurely to conclusions; we need to give the leaders of the Church the benefit of the doubt. The Lord will vindicate the words and works of his anointed servants in time. Of this I have no doubt. In the meantime, we must receive their words, as the revelation declares, "in all patience and faith" (D&C 21:5).

I have no hesitation in acknowledging that I have placed many things on a shelf over the last thirty years. A number of those items have come down from the shelf as information and inspiration have brought light and understanding where darkness and uncertainty had been. Some matters will probably stay on the shelf until that glorious millennial day when the God of heaven makes known those things "which have passed, and hidden things which no man knew, things of the earth, by which it was made, and the purpose and the end thereof—things most precious, things that are above, and things that are beneath, things that are in the earth, and upon the earth, and in heaven" (D&C 101:32–34).

I readily admit that I don't have the answers to all of life's tough questions, questions that are shouted regularly by the dissident as well as the disillusioned: what this doctrine means, why that particular event in our history took place, why this person died so needlessly or that one must endure such terrible suffering. But some things I do know, and I know them through the quiet whisperings of the Holy Ghost: that there is a God and that he is my Father; that there is purpose to life, a reason why we are here and a reason why we experience the things we do; that we can be lifted and cradled by Him who descended below all things and thus understands our plight fully; and that in the end if we will submit to God, surrender our will to him, and trust in his plan and his timetable, we will come to know, in the midst of our earthly challenges, the peace that passes all understanding (Philippians 4:7). If we are able to say, with Job, "Though [God] slay me, yet will I trust in him" (Job 13:15), the shroud of doubt and spiritual darkness will be lifted and removed by the winds of faith and trust in our Redeemer. We then begin to see things as they really are. We can be at peace.

NOTES

1. Conference Report, October 1988, 40.

2. *Doctrines of the Restoration*, 232.

4

Lasting Lessons, Tender Tutorials

At one time or another, every one of us will face adversity, whether it be in the form of financial reversals, personal struggles, the loss of a loved one, or some type of profound disappointment. Adversity will come to us, one and all, whether we are prepared for it or not. Too often in tough times we yield ourselves to stress and distress, to despondency and discouragement, much more than our forebears would have done. Certainly life is more complex, the demands on our time are more intense, and the temptations of the devil are more sophisticated than they were in past ages.

At the same time, it seems to me that there is a mindset, characteristic of our day, that opens us to despair. That mindset is one in which we assume, given all the pleasures and luxuries of our day and age, that all should be well with us, that we should be perpetually happy. Many of us have bought into and imbibed the jargon and the philosophy of our pop psychology world. The fact is, life can be tough. We are not guaranteed a stress-free existence, nor did the Lord promise us a mortal life void of challenge and difficulty.

As we noted earlier, we are now living in a fallen world, one in which things break down, decay, atrophy, and die. We are living in a mortal existence. Now, lest you misunderstand my point, there is much in the world that is glorious and beautiful and uplifting and inspiring; many of the relationships we establish, for example, are elevating and enriching—they bring the deepest of joys into our lives. But we receive sorrow alongside our joys. Both elements of the equation come with the turf, with a life on earth. And we knew this before we came.

C. S. Lewis once observed that God "has paid us the intolerable compliment of loving us, in the deepest, most tragic, most inexorable sense. . . . We are," he continued, "not metaphorically but in very truth, a Divine work of art, something that God is making, and therefore something with which He will not be satisfied until it has a certain character." Thus it is perfectly "natural for us to wish that God had designed for us a less glorious and less arduous destiny; but then we are wishing not for more love but for less."[1] "For whom the Lord loveth he chasteneth, and scourgeth every son whom he receiveth. . . . Now no chastening for the present seemeth to be joyous, but grievous: nevertheless afterward it yieldeth the peaceable fruit of righteousness unto them which are exercised [trained, disciplined] thereby" (Hebrews 12:6, 11). James, the brother of Jesus, therefore instructed us to "count it all joy when ye fall into many afflictions; knowing this, that the trying of your faith worketh patience. But let patience have its perfect work, that ye may be perfect and entire, wanting nothing" (JST James 1:2–4).

In short, there are great lessons to be learned from life's struggles, lessons that can perhaps be acquired in no other way. Many of our afflictions we bring upon ourselves through our own impatience, shortsightedness, or sins. I suppose there are even lessons to be learned from our sins—not the least of which is the motivation to avoid in the future the pain associated with our misdeeds—but these are lessons that I am persuaded the Lord can bring into our lives without our sinning. A man called as a bishop, for example, need not be troubled about the fact that he has lived a faithful life and thus may not be able to feel what the transgressor feels. The Great Physician, he who descended below all things during the awful hours of atonement (D&C 88:6; 122:8), is able, through his Holy Spirit, to reveal to his ordained servants what they need to know and feel in order to lead the wandering sheep back into the fold.

There are, however, lessons that come to us from God through challenges and distresses and setbacks and failures. There is a purifying work of pain, a divine work that can transform the soul of the distressed one, *if* he or she approaches the difficulty with the proper attitude. It is not uncommon for members of the Church who have lost a loved one, or who now must face the prospects of a terminal disease, or whose financial fortunes have been dramatically reversed, to ask: "Why? Why would God do this to me? Why is this happening?" These are, of course, "natural" reactions to trauma, especially when each us would be perfectly content to remain perfectly content! But that's not why we are here.

On more than one occasion I have suggested to the sufferers, as kindly and lovingly as I could, that "Why is this happening?" is not the proper question. Why *is* it happening? Because we are mortal, because things like this happen in a mortal world. No one of us is required by God to enjoy suffering or to anticipate with delight the next trial. I have an associate who said to me once: "You know, Bob, I learn so much from my trials that I find myself praying that the Lord will send more trials my way." I smiled, but I thought to myself: "No way! You wouldn't catch me praying for trials. They come without asking for them."

On the other hand, it makes little sense for us to come to earth to be proven and then to ask why we are being proven. The Father is the Husbandman, the Vinedresser. The Savior is the Vine, and we are the branches. The Vinedresser chooses the manner in which he will purge the branches. Why? "Every branch that beareth fruit," the Master stated, "he [the Father] purgeth it, that it may bring forth more fruit" (John 15:2).

Elder Richard G. Scott pointed out that "when you face adversity, you can be led to ask many questions. Some serve a useful purpose; others do not. To ask, Why does this have to happen to me? Why do I have to suffer this now? What have I done to cause this? will lead you into blind alleys. . . . Rather ask, What am I to do? What am I to learn from this experience? What am I to change? Whom am I to help? How can I remember my many blessings in times of trial?"[2]

In describing life within a prison camp, Victor Frankl has written that "we who lived in concentration camps can remember the men who walked through the huts comforting others, giving away their last piece of bread. They may have been few in number, but they offer sufficient proof that everything can be taken from a man but one thing: the last of . . . human freedoms—to choose one's attitude in any given set of circumstances, [and] to choose one's own way [of life]."[3]

As difficult as it is for me to acknowledge this, we must occasionally be willing to be "broken" if we really expect to gain that broken heart and contrite spirit about which the scriptures speak (Psalms 51:17; 3 Nephi 9:20; D&C 59:8). Inasmuch as our will is the only thing that we can, in the long run, really consecrate to God, the Lord needs to know of our willingness to be broken by him. That is, to what degree are we willing to submit, to surrender, to yield our hearts unto him? "What happens in the breaking of a horse?" someone has asked. "Contrary to what many people believe, the horse's spirit isn't broken. A well-broken horse remains strong, eager, quick-witted, and aware, and he loves to gallop when given free rein. Rather, it is the horse's *independence* that is broken. The breaking of a horse results in the horse giving instant obedience to its rider.

"When a child of God is broken, God does not destroy his or her spirit. We don't lose our zest for living when we come to Christ. We don't lose the force of our personality. Rather, we lose our independence. Our will is brought into submission to the will of the Father so that we can give instant obedience to the one whom we call Savior and Lord. . . .

"We can choose to respond to brokenness with anger, bitterness, and hate. We can rail against our circumstances. We can strike out against those whom we believe have caused us pain. Those options are available to us because we have free will.

"The way to blessing, however, lies in turning to God to heal us and make us whole. We decide whether we will yield to him and trust him."[4]

Indeed, if we approach them properly, our trials can teach and sanctify us, can assist us to know "the fellowship of [Christ's] suffering" (Philippians 3:10). Francis Webster, one of those who suffered unspeakable pain as a member of the Martin Handcart Company, said: "Everyone of us came through with the absolute knowledge that God lives for we became acquainted with him in our extremities."[5]

At a very difficult time for my wife, Shauna, and me—when we watched helplessly as loved ones chose painful and unproductive paths—we found ourselves, early in the process of dealing with the pain, at a crossroads. We sensed, at that early juncture, that our attitude toward what we were experiencing was everything. To be honest, both of us went through a period of weeks and months in which our days were filled with self-doubt, with personal recrimination, with loads of questions about what we had done wrong over the years. But as we prayed with intensity, read scriptures with new and searching eyes, and spent time regularly in the holy temple, there began to distill upon us the quiet but powerful realization that only we could determine how we would deal with our dilemma. Would we allow our problems to strangle our marriage and family? Would we permit these difficulties to drive us into seclusion? Or would we yield to doubt and cynicism, given that we had tried so hard through the years to do what we were asked?

I will be forever grateful that the two of us sensed that we must face this together and that the one thing we could not afford to have happen was for the trial to drive the two of us apart. Further, after a time of being wrung out emotionally and spiritually, we both sensed that the Lord was our only hope for peace, our only means of extricating ourselves from dysfunctional living. It was then that our prayers and our yearnings began to change. It was then that we found ourselves shorn of self-concern and naked in our ineptitude; it was then that we acknowledged our nothingness and drew upon the strength and lifting power of our Divine Redeemer. Oh, we were still concerned, and we kept trying. But we were "trying in a new way, a less worried way."[6]

We should not be unnerved by trials and challenges and even a bad day once in a while. And there are certainly times when a third party, be it a priesthood leader, parent, dear friend, or even a professional counselor, can help us put things in place or in proper perspective. It may even be necessary in some instances for an individual to use medication prescribed by a competent physician. But we must never, ever, minimize the impact the Master can have in our lives, the calming and reassuring and healing balm that he can be to us, no matter the depth of our despair or the seriousness of our situation. "Whatever Jesus lays his hands upon lives," Elder Howard W. Hunter testified. "If Jesus lays his hands upon a marriage, it lives. If he is allowed to lay his hands on the family, it lives."[7]

The touch of the Master's hand is life and light and love. It calms. It soothes. It sanctifies. It empowers. It transcends anything earthly. Those who have been healed by that sacred and sensitive touch are they who can joyously proclaim, like Andrew, Simon Peter's brother, "We have found the Messias" (John 1:41).

I do not wish in any way to minimize some of the tremendous challenges that many of our people face. These are real and sobering. I am very much aware that there are many today who have been subjected to much of pain and distress in their lives, to abuse, to neglect, to the agonies of wanting more than anything to live a normal life and to feel normal feelings, but who seem unable to do so. I would say, first of all, that each one of us, whoever we are, wrestles with something. Perhaps it's things like weight or height or complexion or baldness or I.Q. Perhaps it's problems or issues that pass in time. Perhaps it's the torture of watching helplessly as loved ones choose unwisely and thereby close doors of opportunity for themselves and foreclose future privileges. And then there are the terrible traumas in our life, those occasions when someone we love does despite to our tender trust and deals a blow that strikes at the center of all we hold dear and all we value about ourselves.

I know that the day is coming when all the wrongs, the awful wrongs of this life, will be righted, when the God of justice will attend to all evil. Those things that are beyond our power to control will be corrected, either here or hereafter. Many of us may come to enjoy the lifting, liberating powers of the Atonement in this life, and all our losses will be made up before we pass from this sphere of existence. Perhaps some of us will wrestle all our days with our traumas and our trials, for He who orchestrates the events of our lives will surely fix the time of our release. I have a conviction that when a person passes through the veil of death, all those impediments and challenges and crosses that were beyond his or her power to control—abuse, neglect, immoral environment, weighty traditions, and so forth—will be torn away like a film, and perfect peace will prevail in our hearts.

In some cases our Lord and Master seems to ask of us the impossible—to forgive those who have dreadfully hurt us. As Bruce and Marie Hafen have observed, "That picture somehow has a familiar look—we've seen all this before. Of course, because this picture depicts the sacrifice of Jesus Christ: he took upon himself undeserved and unbearable burdens, heaped upon him by people who often said, and often believed, that they loved him. And he assumed that load not for any need of his, but only to help them.

"So to forgive—not just for abuse victims, but for each of us—is to be a Christ figure, a transitional point in the war between good and evil, stopping the current of evil by absorbing it in every pore, thereby protecting the innocent next generation and helping to enable the repentance and healing of those whose failures sent the jolts into our own systems."[8]

And so we hold on, we press on, we move ahead, even though the road is not necessarily straight and the path is not necessarily clear. Lessons we are to learn through our suffering may or may not be obvious. The one lesson, perhaps overarching all the rest, is patience. Elder Orson F. Whitney taught: "No pain that we suffer, no trial that we experience is wasted. It ministers to our education, to the development of such qualities as patience, faith, fortitude and humility. All that we suffer and all that we endure, especially when we endure it patiently, builds up our characters, purifies our hearts, expands our souls, and makes us more tender and charitable, more worthy to be called the children of God."[9]

At the time Shauna and I were going through some of our deepest sorrows and distresses, we could not have sensed what lessons for life were being chiseled into our souls. It all seemed during that season of stress so overwhelming, so awful, so terribly unfair. And as is true with most of us, it's tough to learn lessons while you're in the midst of the refiner's fire. Now while I would not wish to go through that experience again, at the same time I would not trade the lessons we learned for anything in this world or the next. They were timeless lessons, eternal and tender tutorials that have drawn us closer to the Good Shepherd and expanded our consciousness and empathy for his precious sheep. We learned some things about God during those years of trial, but we also learned some things about ourselves. Fortunately or unfortunately, the only way I can know to what extent I will serve God at all hazards is to have my mettle tested. In asking Abraham to offer his son Isaac, for example, Abraham needed to learn something about Abraham.

In some ways, then, facing our trials courageously and resolutely prepares us for fellowship with those who have passed the tests of mortality. Now, to be sure, The Church of Jesus Christ of Latter-day Saints does not subscribe to a doctrine of asceticism, nor do we teach that we should seek after either persecution or pain. But persecution and pain are the lot of the people of God in all ages, and each of us, saint and sinner alike, becomes acquainted with the Suffering Servant through our own suffering. We have been taught, by those who know best, that "all these things shall give thee experience, and shall be for thy good. The Son of Man hath descended below them all. Art thou greater than he?" (D&C 122:7–8).

No, we are not greater than he, nor should we suppose that fellowship with him who was well acquainted with grief will come through a life of ease. As the apostle Peter counseled us: "Beloved, think it not strange concerning the fiery trial which is to try you, as though some strange thing happened unto you: but rejoice, inasmuch as ye are partakers of Christ's sufferings; that, when his glory shall be revealed, ye may be glad also with exceeding joy" (1 Peter 4:12–13). As tough as it is, over time and through seasons of experience we come to glory in our trials, for only through times of weakness and distress do we eventually emerge into a day of strength and power (2 Corinthians 12:9–10).

NOTES

1. *The Problem of Pain*, 37, 38.

2. Conference Report, October 1995, 18.

3. *Man's Search for Meaning*, 104.

4. Charles Stanley, *The Blessings of Brokenness*, 47–48, 53.

5. Cited in James E. Faust, *Finding Light in a Dark World*, 55.

6. C. S. Lewis, *Mere Christianity*, 131.

7. Conference Report, October 1979, 93.

8. *The Belonging Heart*, 122–23.

9. Cited in Spencer W. Kimball, *Faith Precedes the Miracle*, 98.

OPPOSITION TO THE CHURCH

As we move closer and closer to the end of time, meaning the end of earth's temporal existence, the forces of evil will be combined against the forces of good, particularly the Church of the Lamb of God. A proclamation issued by the Quorum of the Twelve Apostles in April 1845 includes these words: "As this work progresses in its onward course, and becomes more and more an object of political and religious interest and excitement, no king, ruler, or subject, no community or individual, will stand *neutral*. All will at length be influenced by one spirit or the other; and will take sides either for or against the kingdom of God."[1]

Thus we should not be surprised or startled when individuals or whole organizations take issue with or condemn outright the teachings or practices of The Church of Jesus Christ of Latter-day Saints. We have the assurance that there will never again be an apostasy of the Lord's Church, that the kingdom of God is here to stay and will grow and expand to include hundreds of millions of people throughout the earth. Indeed, as Moroni predicted, "Those who are not built upon the Rock will seek to overthrow this church; but it will increase the more opposed."[2]

"We are not without critics," President Gordon B. Hinckley observed, "some of whom are mean and vicious. We have always had them, and I suppose we will have them all through the future. But we shall go forward, returning good for evil, being helpful and kind and generous."[3]

Thus, how we respond to criticism or how we choose to answer hard questions about our faith and way of life are important. This is especially the case as Church membership grows, as temples spread throughout the earth, and as our influence begins to be witnessed and felt more and more.

Most people around us like the way we live and even like the way we talk. But they're just plain uncomfortable with the doctrine that underlies our behavior. In point of fact, however, our conduct and our way of life cannot be separated from our doctrine, for what we believe empowers and directs what we do. A number of years ago an article appeared in *Christianity Today* entitled "Why Your Neighbor Joined the Mormon Church." Five reasons were given:

1. The Latter-day Saints show genuine love and concern by taking care of their people.
2. They strive to build the family unit.
3. They provide for their young people.
4. Theirs is a layman's church.
5. They believe that divine revelation is the basis for their practices.

After a brief discussion of each item on the list, the author of the article concluded: "In a day when many are hesitant to claim that God has said anything definitive, the Mormons stand out in contrast, and many people are ready to listen to what the Mormons think the voice of God says. It is tragic that their message is false, but it is nonetheless a lesson to us that people are many times ready to hear a voice of authority."[4]

The Savior taught of the importance of judging things—prophets, for example—by their fruits, by the product of their ministry and teachings (Matthew 7:15–20). He also explained that "every plant, which my heavenly Father hath not planted, shall be rooted up" (Matthew 15:13). Evil trees cannot bring forth good fruit. Works of men eventually come to naught, but that which is of God cannot be overthrown (Acts 5:38–39).

In encountering those who pose questions to us—either sincere or curious investigators on the one hand or critics of the Church on the other—there are certain simple but worthwhile observations to consider. First, all of us can have sufficient knowledge and testimony of the gospel to sustain and defend the faith; no formal schooling or training is necessary, although we are always in a better position to provide a reason for the hope within us (1 Peter 3:15) when we have become more than distant acquaintances of the doctrines of the gospel. Second, while we want to be helpful where we can, we are not obligated to provide answers to everyone's questions. In fact, some questions are best not answered (Alma 11:21–22). The Lord has not yet answered all of my questions, and I rather suspect he hasn't cleared up all of yours either. Third, as Latter-day Saints, we already know more about God and Christ and the plan of salvation than anyone who might seek to deter us from a faithful course. We need to be confident and assured in the knowledge that is ours.

Let me also share three suggestions—learned through both sad and sweet experience—on how we might effectively deal with difficult questions posed by those not of our faith. First, *stay in control of yourself.* There is nothing more frustrating than knowing the truth, loving the truth, sincerely desiring to share the truth, and yet being unable to communicate our deepest feelings to another who sees things differently. Argument or disputation over sacred things causes us to forfeit the Spirit of God and thus the confirming power of our message (3 Nephi 11:28–30). We teach and we testify. Contention is unbecoming of one called to publish peace and thus bless our brothers and sisters. In the words of Elder Marvin J. Ashton, "We have no time for contention. We only have time to be about our Father's business."[5]

In 1896 President Joseph F. Smith wrote to one of his missionary sons: "Kindness will beget friendship and favor, but anger or passion will drive away sympathy. To win one's respect and confidence, approach them mildly, kindly. No friendship was ever gained by an attack upon principle or upon man, but by calm reason and the lowly Spirit of Truth. If you have built for a man a better house than his own, and he is willing to accept yours and forsake his, then, and not till then, should you proceed to tear down the old structure. Rotten though it may be, it will require some time for it to lose *all* its charms and fond memories of its former occupant. Therefore let *him,* not *you,* proceed to tear it away. Kindness and courtesy are the primal elements of gentility."[6]

I have been a student of the Book of Mormon for many years, and I have come to value its pages, its principles, and its precepts more than silver or gold. But, like you, I continue to discover new truths and new applications with new readings and new experiences in life. For example, I have read the first chapter of Alma many, many times. But in recent years a particular reading of the text brought to light a lesson, a stern warning. In speaking of what took place in about 90 B.C., Mormon explains: "It came to pass that whosoever did not belong to the church of God began to persecute those that did belong to the church of God, and had taken upon them the name of Christ. Yea, they did persecute them, and afflict them with all manner of words." He notes that "there was a strict law among the people of the church, that there should not any man, belonging to the church, arise and persecute those that did not belong to the church, and that there should be no persecution among themselves.

"Nevertheless," Mormon adds, "there were many among them"—meaning the church—"who began to be proud, and began to contend warmly with their adversaries, even unto blows; yea, they would smite one another with their fists." (Parenthetically, I would confess that I've been involved in some pretty heated discussions on religious topics, but I have never been in a fist fight!) Mormon points out that these unfortunate instances were the cause of "much trial with the church." Why? Consider the next verse: "For the hearts of many were hardened, and their names were blotted out, that they were remembered no more among the people of God. And also many withdrew themselves from among them" (Alma 1:19–24). How tragic! Here we have members of the Church of Jesus Christ whose contention for the faith cost them their faith and their membership.

Second, *stay in order.* The Savior taught that gospel prerequisites should be observed when teaching sacred things (Matthew 7:6–7).[7]

A person, for example, who knows very little about our doctrine will probably not understand or appreciate our teachings concerning temples, sealing powers, eternal life, or the deification of man. The Prophet Joseph Smith explained that "if we start right, it is easy to go right all the time; but if we start wrong, we may go wrong, and it [will] be a hard matter to get right."[8]

It is always wise to lay a proper foundation for what is to be said; the truth can then flow more freely.

Let me illustrate. After I had been on a mission for about fifteen months, I was assigned to work in a beautiful section of Connecticut. My companion, a nice fellow to be sure, had one particular problem that affected the work somewhat—his mind was never with us. He was always off in another world, or so it seemed. We came to the door of a small but lovely home. I can still remember what a beautiful day it was, in the early summer of the year. It was Elder Jackson's turn to be the spokesman. A woman who appeared to be about thirty-five years old opened her door and unlatched the screen door. She said: "Yes. Is there something I can do for you?"

My companion answered: "We're missionaries for The Church of Jesus Christ of Latter-day Saints. We have a message about Christ that we would like to share with you."

She looked us over very carefully. Then she responded: "I don't think so. I have my own faith."

My companion, who probably wasn't paying attention to what she said, went silent. After waiting uncomfortably for at least ten or fifteen seconds, I blurted out: "And what church do you attend?"

She came right back: "I didn't say I attended a church; I said that I had my own faith."

Somewhat surprised, I said: "Could you tell us about your faith?"

She said: "I don't think I want to. You would make fun of me."

I assured her that we would not make fun of her. "What is your faith?" I asked.

"Well," she timidly declared, "I believe the physical body is the temple of God and that people ought to take better care of their bodies. For example, I think it's wrong for people to smoke or drink." I commented that we felt her thinking was right on the mark. She continued: "Well, there's more. I don't drink coffee or tea." Then she asked: "What do the Mormons believe?"

It was difficult for me not to speak out, but I felt I ought to allow Elder Jackson to engage what was obviously a great teaching moment. He stood erect, and I could almost see the wheels in his mental machinery turning. He answered: "Well, we believe in baptism for the dead."

The woman carefully pulled the screen door shut and latched it. Before closing the main door she said, with a pained look on her face, "That sounds sick."

I had some idea of what she was thinking and of how bizarre these Latter-day Saints appeared to be. Mostly I was stunned, shocked. Before we left the porch, I turned to Elder Jackson and asked in utter disbelief: "What are you doing?"

He seemed offended and said: "We do believe in baptism for the dead, don't we?"

I said, "Yes, we do, Elder Jackson. Why didn't you tell her about polygamy?"

His response was even more stunning: "I thought about doing that next, but she closed the door."

"Elder," I said, "this lady lives the Word of Wisdom."

"I thought that was odd," he added, as we walked to the next door.

This woman had essentially come to the door with her cup and said, "I thirst." We had answered, "We can fix that," and then proceeded to drag out the fire hose and drown her in the living waters. It isn't that this woman was not bright enough to understand the concept of salvation for the dead. The problem was that we had not laid a proper doctrinal foundation, and our message therefore seemed to be spoken against reason. There is indeed a system of gospel prerequisites.

Third, *stay in context*. We love the Bible and cherish its messages. But the Bible is not the source of our doctrine or authority, nor is much to be gained through efforts to "prove" the truthfulness of the restored gospel from the Bible. Ours is an independent revelation. We know what we know about the premortal existence, priesthood, celestial marriage, baptism for the dead, the postmortal spirit world, degrees of glory, and so forth, because of what God has made known through latter-day prophets, not because we are able to identify a few biblical allusions to these matters.

Some of our greatest difficulties in handling questions about our faith come when we try to establish specific doctrines of the Restoration from the Bible alone. We have an obligation—a sacred obligation—to rely upon the Book of Mormon, the Doctrine and Covenants, the Pearl of Great Price, the Joseph Smith Translation of the Bible, and especially the teachings of latter-day apostles and prophets, in establishing our doctrine. There is consummate peace and spiritual power to be derived from being loyal and true to those things the Almighty has communicated to us in our dispensation (D&C 5:10; 31:3–4; 43:15–16; 49:1–4; 84:54–61).

In September 1832 the Lord warned of a condemnation, a scourge, and a judgment that would rest upon the whole Church until we took seriously the Book of Mormon and the revelations of the Restoration (D&C 84:54–61). In short, there is a loyalty that should and must exist among us, a loyalty to those things the Lord has given to us. We are commanded to "declare glad tidings." And what are those tidings? Are we to go into the world and reteach the Sermon on the Mount, the Bread of Life sermon, or any of those remarkable doctrines contained in the New Testament? As we have said before, we cherish the Bible and seek to safeguard its truths, but we are called upon, in the words of the Lord, to "declare the things which have been revealed to my servant, Joseph Smith, Jun." (D&C 31:3–4).

While we seek to make friends and build bridges of understanding where possible, we do not court favor, nor do we compromise one whit on what we believe. Some doctrines, like the doctrine of "the only true and living church" (D&C 1:30), by their very nature, arouse antagonism from those of other faiths. Would it not be wise, some have asked, to avoid or at least downplay such divisive points? Perhaps, some say, we should consider focusing on matters we have in common and put aside, for the time being, the distinctive teachings of the Restoration. Elder Boyd K. Packer declared: "If we thought only in terms of diplomacy or popularity, surely we should change our course.

"But we must hold tightly to it even though some turn away. . . .

"It is not an easy thing for us to defend the position that bothers so many others.

"Brethren and sisters, never be ashamed of the gospel of

Jesus Christ. Never apologize for the sacred doctrines of the gospel.

"Never feel inadequate and unsettled because you cannot explain them to the satisfaction of all who might inquire of you.

"Do not be ill at ease or uncomfortable because you can give little more than your conviction. . . .

"If we can stand without shame, without hesitancy, without embarrassment, without reservation to bear witness that the gospel has been restored, that there are prophets and Apostles upon the earth, that the truth is available for all mankind, the Lord's Spirit will be with us. And that assurance can be affirmed to others."[9]

President Gordon B. Hinckley declared: "If we will go forward, never losing sight of our goal, speaking ill of no one, living the great principles we know to be true, this cause will roll on in majesty and power to fill the earth. Doors now closed to the preaching of the gospel will be opened. The Almighty, if necessary, may have to shake the nations to humble them and cause them to listen to the servants of the living God. Whatever is needed will come to pass."[10]

This work is true, and because it is true it will triumph. The destiny of the restored kingdom is set, and we need not fear for the success of the Church. The repeated plea in scripture is "Fear not." The promise of Deity is encouraging and strengthening to our faith: "Verily, thus saith the Lord unto you—there is no weapon that is formed against you shall prosper; and if any man lift his voice against you he shall be confounded in mine own due time. Wherefore, keep my commandments; they are true and faithful. Even so. Amen" (D&C

71:9–11; compare 136:17). God will bring to pass his purposes; of that we can rest assured.

NOTES

1. *Messages of the First Presidency*, 1:257; emphasis in original.
2. This prophecy was included among the teachings and instructions Moroni gave to Joseph Smith on 21 and 22 September 1823, as recorded in a letter Oliver Cowdery wrote to W. W. Phelps, published in *The Latter-day Saints' Messenger and Advocate*, 2:199.
3. Conference Report, April 2001, 4.
4. Donald P. Shoemaker, "Why Your Neighbor Joined the Mormon Church," 11–13.
5. Conference Report, April 1978, 9.
6. Letter to Hyrum M. Smith, 18 May 1896, in Smith, *From Prophet to Son*, 42–43; emphasis in original.
7. See also Boyd K. Packer, *Teach Ye Diligently*, chapter 11; *The Holy Temple*, chapter 2.
8. *Teachings of the Prophet Joseph Smith*, 343.
9. Conference Report, October 1985, 104, 107.
10. Conference Report, October 1997, 92.

6

FALSE CHRISTS AND
FALSE PROPHETS

In his Olivet discourse, the Savior warned his disciples of false Christs and false prophets (Matthew 24:24; Joseph Smith–Matthew 1:22). With the exception of a few deluded individuals who claim messianic authority, false Christs are generally false systems of salvation, errant paths to happiness and peace here and eternal reward hereafter. False prophets are those who seek to deceive, "who use the name of the Lord, and use it in vain, having not authority" (D&C 63:62). False prophets are "teachers and preachers who profess to speak for the Lord when, in fact, they have received no such appointment. . . . They are teachers of religion who do not receive revelation and have not gained from the Holy Ghost the true testimony of Jesus." They "are false teachers; they teach false doctrine; they neither know nor teach the doctrines of salvation."[1]

While few of us in the restored Church are led astray to such extent that we acknowledge one as having divine authority when he does not, too often we are captivated and captured by those claiming some new insight, some novel interpretation of prophecy, some easier way to God and unusual spiritual experiences. We need not defect to full-scale apostasy to dilute our discipleship; we need only give an ear or

lend our undivided attention to a cause, a crusade, or a movement that is not ordained of God and not in harmony with the
teachings of the Church and its constituted authorities. Alma
counseled us to "trust no one to be your teacher nor your minister, except he be a man of God, walking in his ways and
keeping his commandments" (Mosiah 23:14).

In the first few centuries following the death of Christ
there grew up a movement that came to be known as
Gnosticism. The word *gnosis* connoted for them knowledge,
not a general kind of knowledge, but rather a special, saving
knowledge. The Gnostics were a group who claimed to be pos-
sessors of the esoteric teachings of Jesus, the supposedly sacred
and secret messages reserved only for those who sought to rise
above the mundane and liberate themselves from the fetters of
ignorance and a confining physical world. They decried and
defied, for the most part, what they believed to be a stifling
and restrictive priesthood hierarchy of the orthodox church.
Salvation was an individual experience that came through
spiritual illumination of the mysteries of godliness.

In the times of restitution, we have not been without our
own little Gnostic groups. There was Hiram Page, who sought
to reveal things about Zion (D&C 28); Mrs. Hubble, who
claimed to be receiving divine direction for the Saints (D&C
43); some who spoke of secret commissions and ordinations
under the hands of Joseph Smith; and others today who make
much of special callings or unusual insights. We have watched
with much interest and pain as a surprising number of the
Lord's people are lured away by voices that beckon for their
attention. Safety and security in the midst of a babble of voices
are to be found in following the Brethren, in giving heed to
the counsel and direction we receive from our leaders at the

general conferences of the Church and in the official organs and publications of the Church. When we are loyal to this principle, we would never seek to run ahead of our file leaders, to suggest that the Saints should do this or that when in fact those responsible for guiding the destiny of the Church and kingdom have not so spoken.[2]

The Lord does not ask us to magnify other people's callings.

Few people would go astray, would find themselves in apostasy or in the center of controversy, if they simply sought for and followed the counsel of their Church leaders. People are not necessarily called to positions of responsibility because they are the most qualified, the most talented, or the best informed. Our challenge is to sustain—that is, give our full loyalty and support to—people who are often less than perfect, even people that we might feel to be less capable than ourselves. "You can put it down in your little black book," Elder Boyd K. Packer taught, "that if you will not be loyal in the small things, you will not be loyal in the large things. . . .

"A man who says he will sustain the President of the Church or the General Authorities, but cannot sustain his own bishop, is deceiving himself. The man who will not sustain the bishop of his ward and the president of his stake will not sustain the President of the Church."[3]

There are ways of knowing the truth, of discerning the veracity and fruitfulness of a doctrine or a point of view. The Prophet Joseph Smith pointed out that nothing is a greater injury to the children of men than to be under the influence of a false spirit when we suppose we have the Spirit of God.[4]

If someone comes to us claiming a special appointment, special knowledge that is not available to most members, special training and abilities that entitle him or her to interpret scripture, clarify doctrine, or chart a course beyond what has been given by the authorized servants of God, we might ask the following:

Is the person claiming a divine communication or insight acting within the bounds of his or her respective assignment? The Lord's house is a house of order, not of confusion (D&C 132:8). Chaos would ensue rather quickly if every person were permitted to receive revelations or provide divine direction for every other person in the Church, irrespective of stewardship. The Prophet taught, for example, that "it is contrary to the economy of God" for people to receive revelation for those higher in authority than themselves.[5]

He also explained that it is "the privilege of any officer in this Church to obtain revelations, so far as [it] relates to his particular calling and duty in the Church."[6] There is order. There are proper channels.

Is the recipient of the communication worthy to receive the same? Though we may not always be in a position to judge another's worthiness, we are generally pretty good judges of our own. The revelations indicate that the works of God are brought to pass through those who are clean, who have been purified from the sins of the world (3 Nephi 8:1; D&C 50:28). God will generally not work through polluted channels. In fact, President Harold B. Lee offered the following sobering remarks: "We get our answers from the source of the power we list to obey. If we're following the ways of the devil, we'll get answers from the devil. If we're keeping the commandments of God, we'll get our answers from God."[7]

Is the communication in harmony with the teachings of the standard works and those of the living oracles? When people claim to have received word that they should join a polygamous cult or participate in a demonic practice or be disloyal or disobedient to the government, one wonders how they can justify their position. When others indicate that they have been directed by the Lord to lie or cheat or steal or be immoral, one wonders how such actions can square with the teachings of the Church. Often individuals claim that their case is an exception to the rule. We would do well as a people to stay within the rules and avoid the exceptions, especially when such exceptions stand in violation of the law and order of the kingdom of God. Those still convinced that what they are commanded to do is of God would do well to counsel with their priesthood leaders and then follow that counsel emphatically.

Does the communication edify or instruct? Is it consistent with the dignity that should attend something that comes from the Almighty? If a supposed communication from heaven dictates that someone act foolish or undignified or yield themselves completely to erratic behavior or emotional display, then we ought to question the veracity of the communication. The Prophet Joseph Smith explained that in the early days of the Church "many ridiculous things were entered into, calculated [by Satan] to bring disgrace upon the Church of God, to cause the Spirit of God to be withdrawn, and to uproot and destroy those glorious principles which had been developed for the salvation of the human family." He stated an important principle when he said: "There is nothing unnatural in the Spirit of God."[8]

Does the communication build our faith and commitment to the kingdom of God and strengthen our loyalty to its constituted authorities? There is a litmus test that can be applied, a vital criterion that must be met if a supposed revelation is from God. We ask such questions as the following: Does this communication strengthen my faith in Joseph Smith and the Restoration? Do I feel more motivated to serve faithfully in the Church and kingdom? Does this manifestation build my confidence in the Lord's anointed servants today and in the destiny of the Church? God does not and will not work against himself; he will not confuse his people by having them believe or do things that would in any way weaken their hold on the iron rod.

The Lord set forth a pattern for the Saints to observe, a guide in determining whom we should follow and to whose words we should give heed: "I say unto you, that it shall not be given to any one to go forth to preach my gospel, or to build up my church, except he be ordained by some one who has authority, and it is known to the church that he has authority and has been regularly ordained by the heads of the church" (D&C 42:11). After having cited this passage, Elder Boyd K. Packer lifted a warning voice: "There are some among us now who have *not* been regularly ordained by the heads of the Church and who tell of impending political and economic chaos, the end of the world—something of the 'sky is falling, chicken licken' of the fables. They are misleading members to gather to colonies or cults.

"Those deceivers say that the Brethren do not know what is going on in the world or that the Brethren approve of their teaching but do not wish to speak of it over the pulpit. Neither is true. The Brethren, by virtue of traveling constantly everywhere on earth, certainly know what is going on and by virtue of prophetic insight are able to read the signs of the times.

"Do not be deceived by them—those deceivers. If there is to be any gathering, it will be announced by those who have been regularly ordained and who are known to the Church to have authority.

"Come away from any others. Follow your leaders, who have been duly ordained and have been publicly sustained, and you will not be led astray."[9]

Truly, "False prophets always arise to oppose the true prophets and they will prophesy so very near the truth that they will deceive almost the very chosen ones."[10]

No true believer wants to be deceived, to be led astray. No disciple of Christ wants to waste his or her time and energy and zeal on a secondary cause or a misguided effort. All of us desire to stay true to the faith, "true to the truth for which martyrs have perished,"[11] true to the end. But each of us knows that Satan's tactics and his teachings are becoming ever more sophisticated and seductive. Wherein is safety? How can we discern the lies of the father of lies?

A fascinating pattern for discernment is found in the first chapter of the book of Moses. This remarkable chapter records an experience of Moses the Lawgiver that is found nowhere else in scripture, an inspiring account of Moses' face to face encounter with God and his vision of the earth and all of its inhabitants, past, present, and future. Also found here is an account of Moses' encounter with Satan and the latter's strategy to confuse and confound Moses. For one thing, it is worth noting that Satan appeared after Moses had seen God, after "he was left unto himself" and in the weakness of his mortality had fallen "unto the earth. And it came to pass that it was for the space of many hours before Moses did again receive his natural strength like unto man" (Moses 1:9–10). In short, the arch-deceiver came onto the scene, as he so often does with us, when the prophet was at his weakest.

As seasoned and versatile as the devil is, however, Moses had an advantage: he had stood in the very presence of God, was nourished and enlivened by his Spirit, and came to know who he (Moses) was and his place in the plan of God. That is, Moses had gained an elevated perspective and also had felt the power of God and entered the realm of divine experience. Thus, when he was approached by another who demanded his worship, Moses replied: "Who art thou? For behold, I am a son of God, in the similitude of his Only Begotten; and where is thy glory, that I should worship thee?" (Moses 1:12–13).

In short, the more experience a person has with God and with the Spirit of God, the more readily he or she is able to discern and dismiss false Christs and false prophets. The Holy Ghost is thus the key to our discernment, the vital key to our capacity to distinguish false spirits—false persons, doctrines, and ideas—from that which is ordained and sent forth by God. Our hope for survival in the midst of competing and, in some cases, compelling voices will be realized to the extent that we seek the Spirit, follow the Brethren, and stay in the main-stream of the Church. Therein is safety.

NOTES

1. Bruce R. McConkie, *The Millennial Messiah,* 70–71.

2. See Joseph F. Smith, *Gospel Doctrine,* 185.

3. "Follow the Brethren," 4–5.

4. *Teachings of the Prophet Joseph Smith,* 205.

5. *Teachings of the Prophet Joseph Smith,* 21.

6. *Teachings of the Prophet Joseph Smith,* 111.

7. *Stand Ye in Holy Places,* 138.

8. *Teachings of the Prophet Joseph Smith,* 214; see also 203–4, 209.

9. Conference Report, October 1992, 102; emphasis in original.

10. *Teachings of the Prophet Joseph Smith,* 365.

11. Evan Stephens, "True to the Faith," in *Hymns of The Church of Jesus Christ of Latter-day Saints,* no. 254.

7

WARS AND RUMORS OF WARS

The Prophet Joseph Smith learned that with the advent of what we know as the War between the States, "war will be poured out upon all nations, beginning at this place [South Carolina]." The Lord then spoke of the expanding influence of war, about slaves rising up against their masters, about coalitions during major world wars, and about bloodshed, famine, and plague, "until the consumption decreed hath made a full end of all nations." The prophecy on war ends with this solid counsel: "Wherefore, stand ye in holy places, and be not moved, until the day of the Lord come; for behold, it cometh quickly, saith the Lord. Amen" (D&C 87:2–8).

War, it seems, is forever with us. Indeed, war historians acknowledge that since the 1860s there has not been a time when war of some sort was not underway on this earth. That war comes upon us because of human selfishness is clear from scripture. "From whence come wars and fightings among you?" James asked. "Come they not hence, even of your lusts that war in your members? Ye lust, and have not: ye kill, and desire to have, and cannot obtain: ye fight and war, yet ye have not, because ye ask not. Ye ask, and receive not, because ye ask amiss [wickedly, wrongly], that ye may consume it upon your lusts." James went on to say that "the Spirit that dwelleth in us lusteth to envy. But [God] giveth more grace. Wherefore he saith, God resisteth the proud, but giveth grace unto the humble" (James 4:1–3, 5–6). The spread of organized conflict in the form of war is thus an indication of fallen man's having yielded to his own carnal nature.

Because it is the case, as the revelations indicate, that war will be with us until the King of kings comes to earth to settle all disputes and bring peace, we would be well-advised to learn how to deal with the issue of war most productively and positively. Using the Book of Mormon as our guide, let us consider the following suggestions:

1. *Understand what war really is.* "War is basically selfish," President David O. McKay stated. "Its roots feed in the soil of envy, hatred, desire for domination. Its fruit, therefore, is always bitter. . . .

"War impels you to hate your enemies.

"The Prince of Peace says, Love your enemies.

"War says, Curse them that curse you.

"The Prince of Peace says, Pray for them that curse you.

"War says, Injure and kill them that hate you.

"The Risen Lord says, Do good to them that hate you. . . .

"The gospel of Jesus Christ is the gospel of peace. . . . There are, however, two conditions which may justify a truly Christian man to enter—mind you, I say *enter, not begin*—a war: (1) An attempt to dominate and deprive another of his free agency, and, (2) Loyalty to his country. Possibly there is a third, viz., Defense of a weak nation that is being unjustly crushed by a strong, ruthless one. . . .

"To deprive an intelligent human being of his free agency is to commit the crime of the ages. . . .

"So fundamental in man's eternal progress is his inherent

right to choose, that the Lord would defend it even at the price of war. Without freedom of thought, freedom of choice, freedom of action within lawful bounds, man cannot progress."[1]

It was in that spirit, in fact, that the righteous Nephite military leaders led their people into war. First of all, they entered war to protect their families and their civil and religious liberties, feeling that this was an obligation they owed to God, as well as their people. Theirs was never an offensive war—they understood that offensive war would not entitle them to the blessings of heaven (Alma 43:9–10, 44–47; 48:14–15; 3 Nephi 3:20–21; compare D&C 98:23–36).

2. *Be supportive of constituted government.* In our day the Lord has instructed us that Latter-day Saints in the United States are to be subject to the powers that be until Christ reigns as King of kings (D&C 58:21–22; 134:1, 5). Though some of Captain Moroni's actions might be bothersome to the more pacifistic of this modern age, he acted in harmony with what he felt was his and others' duty to God, even to the point of compelling dissenters to take up arms in support of the government during times of war (Alma 51:15–16). At those times when he sensed that moral support for government or the cause of liberty was waning, Moroni single-handedly sought to foster enthusiasm and engender support for the government by reminding the people of their promises to God. This was the essence of the "Title of Liberty" episode. That incident was more than a large pep rally, more than an emotional appeal; it was a covenant-renewal ceremony in which this mighty prophet-leader called upon the people to remember their duty to God, duty to church, duty to country, and duty to one another as Christians. We thus pray earnestly for those who represent us in government and take our own responsibilities as citizens seriously.

3. *Be faithful. Righteousness in society is fundamental.* For the faithful Nephites, righteousness was at the heart of good government; a government was only as good as its people and its leaders. They were convinced that they could enjoy the blessings and protection of the Almighty only in a state of faithfulness and fidelity to their covenants (Alma 46:22). In our day and through the Prophet Joseph Smith, we learn: "I, the Lord God, make you free, therefore ye are free indeed; and the law also maketh you free. Nevertheless, when the wicked rule the people mourn. Wherefore, honest men and wise men should be sought for diligently, and good men and wise men ye should observe to uphold" (D&C 98:8–10).

In speaking of America, Moroni observed: "Behold, this is a choice land, and whatsoever nation shall possess it shall be free from bondage, and from captivity, and from all other nations under heaven, if they will but serve the God of the land, who is Jesus Christ" (Ether 2:12). This is why, no matter how much we might make our influence for good felt in society, the most fundamental and enduring difference we can make in the world will come through teaching the principles of the restored gospel. Having paid high praise to Captain Moroni, Mormon added this important detail, a powerful statement about what good people can and should do during times of war: "Now behold, Helaman and his brethren were no less serviceable unto the people than was Moroni; for they did preach the word of God, and they did baptize unto repentance all men whosoever would hearken unto their words" (Alma 48:19). Indeed, as Alma noted, the preaching of the word has "a great tendency to lead the people to do that which [is] just." In fact, it has a more powerful impact "than the sword, or anything else" (Alma 31:5).

As Elder Bruce R. McConkie testified: "I maintain that the

most beneficial and productive thing which Latter-day Saints can do to strengthen every good and proper cause is to live and teach the principles of the everlasting gospel.

"There may be those who have special gifts and needs to serve in other fields, but as far as I am concerned, with the knowledge and testimony that I have, there is nothing I can do for the time and season of this mortal probation, that is more important than to use all my strength, energy and ability in spreading and perfecting the cause of truth and righteousness, both in the Church and among our Father's other children."[2]

4. *Be positive. Be optimistic. Our circumstances and surroundings need not determine our behavior or our attitude toward daily life.* One need not be a Pollyanna about life in order to be optimistic about living in difficult times. Rather, we need simply to realize that moaning and groaning and complaining about the evil of our day will do little to improve the world.

Remarkably good things can and do take place during times of crisis. It was during the period of wars that Alma was taken from the midst of the people, presumably translated and taken from the earth without tasting death (Alma 45:8–19). Oddly enough, Mormon writes of a time during the days of Nephite wars when, because of the steadiness of the members of the Church, "they did prosper exceedingly, and they became exceedingly rich; yea, and they did multiply and wax strong in the land. And thus we see how merciful and just are all the dealings of the Lord, to the fulfilling of all his words unto the children of men. . . . Behold, there never was a happier time among the people of Nephi, since the days of Nephi, than in the days of Moroni" (Alma 50:18–19, 23).

Indeed, the Nephite record provides a profound lesson about how one responds to his or her circumstances. Note this language about the end of the wars: "And thus ended the thirty and first year of the reign of the judges over the people of Nephi; and thus they had had wars, and bloodsheds, and famine, and affliction, for the space of many years. And there had been murders, and contentions, and dissensions, and all manner of iniquity among the people of Nephi; nevertheless for the righteous' sake, yea, because of the prayers of the righteous, they were spared. But behold, because of the exceedingly great length of the war between the Nephites and the Lamanites many had become hardened, . . . and many were softened because of their afflictions, insomuch that they did humble themselves before God, even in the depth of humility" (Alma 62:39–41). How they reacted to pain, to distress, to heartache, to strife in society was a personal choice.

A bit of perspective on the future may be helpful here. While we know that wars and bloodshed and gross wickedness will characterize much of the planet until the initiation of the millennial reign, we also know that consummate righteousness and peace will be found among the Saints of the Most High. That is, while the mother of abominations spreads her nefarious influence throughout the four corners of the earth, the Church of the Lamb will spread a righteous influence, albeit on a smaller scale. "And it came to pass that I, Nephi, beheld the power of the Lamb of God, that it descended upon the saints of the church of the Lamb, and upon the covenant people of the Lord, who were scattered upon all the face of the earth; and they were armed with righteousness and with the power of God in great glory" (1 Nephi 14:11–14).

While tears and tests and trials lie ahead, there is so very much to look forward to: the spread of the restored gospel to all the world, temples dotting the earth, Latter-day Saints providing a leavening influence in the arts, sciences, education, and the entertainment industry. There is so much for us to have faith in, not the least of which is the future of the United States of America. "Men may fail in this country," President Harold B. Lee affirmed to Ricks College students in 1973, "earthquakes may come, seas may heave beyond their bounds, there may be great drought, disaster, and hardship, but this nation, founded on principles laid down by men whom God raised up, will never fail. This is the cradle of humanity, where life on this earth began in the Garden of Eden. This is the place of the new Jerusalem. . . . I have faith in America; you and I must have faith in America, if we understand the teachings of the gospel of Jesus Christ. . . .

"I plead with you not to preach pessimism. Preach that this is the greatest country in all the world. This is the favored land. This is the land of our forefathers. It is the nation that will stand despite whatever trials or crises it may yet have to pass through."[3]

While we must, on the one hand, be fully aware of the evils of our time, ever vigilant to the creeping corruption and raging relativism of the day, we must not allow ourselves to become prey to that cynicism that is an enemy to spirituality. It was just after the uncovering of the scandal of Watergate that Elder Bruce R. McConkie lifted his voice to the members of the Church. "There is an eternal law," he said, "ordained by God himself before the foundations of the world, that every man shall reap as he sows. If we think evil thoughts, our tongues will utter unclean sayings. If we speak words of wickedness, we shall end up doing the works of wickedness. If our minds are centered on the carnality and evil of the world, then worldliness and unrighteousness will seem to us to be the normal way of life. If we ponder things related to sex immorality in our minds, we will soon think everybody is immoral and unclean and it will break down the barrier between us and the world. . . .

"On the other hand, if we are pondering in our hearts the things of righteousness, we shall become righteous."[4]

A passage of scripture that has special appeal to me is from the writings of the apostle Paul: "Whatsoever things are true, whatsoever things are honest, whatsoever things are just, whatsoever things are pure, whatsoever things are lovely, whatsoever things are of good report; *if there be any virtue, and if there be any praise, think on these things*" (Philippians 4:8; emphasis added). Paul states that we are to think on—that is, focus upon—things that are true, honest, just, pure, lovely, of good report, virtuous, and praiseworthy. While we are not to be naïve in regard to evil or foolish in regard to unholy influences about us, we are not to fixate upon them or conclude that all is lost. There is too much good to be seen and acknowledged, too much good to be enjoyed and appreciated, too much good to be accomplished by those bent on the salvation of souls. We have no time for despair, no time for feeling sorry for ourselves; we only have time to be about our Father's business. There's a world out there waiting to be saved.

NOTES

1. Conference Report, April 1942, 70–73; emphasis in original.

2. Conference Report, October 1973, 55.

3. *Ye Are the Light of the World*, 350–51.

4. Conference Report, October 1973, 56.

8

THINGS OUT OF OUR CONTROL

A dear friend shared with me the pain associated with a wandering child. He explained that their youngest daughter had, over a period of months, begun to change her social circle and develop new acquaintances. In the process she began to drift into forbidden territory, including serious violations of the law of chastity and the Word of Wisdom. Her engagement with drugs initiated her into a dark world of organized crime among men and women who would literally do anything to appease their cravings and satisfy their habit.

As he spoke of this tragic time in his daughter's life, he wept as he told of long months where there was no word, no contact with her, no idea whether she was dead or alive. He remarked how often he and his wife had spent almost whole nights on their knees, pleading with a loving Lord to reach out, preserve, and return their precious one to them. My friend stated, in essence: "There's no way to describe the feelings of utter helplessness associated with not knowing where she was—whether lying in a ditch beside the road, in a flop house somewhere, or at the bottom of a lake. It was a situation that was out of our hands, completely beyond our control. There was so little, so very little that we could do."

Much of life is out of our hands. There are some things that we simply can't do a thing to change. Consider the following examples:

For almost all of us, we have no control whatsoever over the *economy*. We can choose to live frugally and within our means, invest wisely and conservatively, and make appropriate financial plans for the future; but in the end such matters as the interest rate, the cost of housing, and the price of gasoline and other fundamental commodities are items outside our immediate control.

How much control do you or I have over whether our country is involved in *war*, whether young people are drafted into military service, whether we are asked to cut back on our consumption of certain products especially crucial to the war effort? In recent times we as Americans (and, for that matter, a worldwide community) have been sobered by the fact that though we can certainly exercise cautions in our travel and cooperate with governmental regulations concerning security, we literally have no control over whether some crazed and bloodthirsty person boards a plane and chooses to kill all those aboard.

Nothing is more common to mortals than *death*; it is the common lot of all who come into this life to leave it. Every man or woman is born, and every man or woman must die. All are born as helpless infants, and all depart this sphere equally helpless in the face of death. Death is something most of us fear, something from which we hide, something most of us would avoid if we could. Even among those who read by the lamp of gospel understanding, death is frequently viewed with fear and trembling. While we know, more surely than any other people on earth, of the reality of the immortality of the soul and of the promise of a joyful reunion with departed loved ones, yet we hedge, we hold back, we hesitate when it comes to letting the loved one go. The same is true of our own lives. We can strive to eat properly, exercise regularly, and get adequate rest, but eventually, and usually at an unexpected hour, the grim reaper of death invades our premises.

Nor do we have complete control over *spiritual things* in our lives. Jesus said to Nicodemus: "The wind bloweth where it listeth, and thou hearest the sound thereof, but canst not tell whence it cometh, and whither it goeth: so is every one that is born of the Spirit" (John 3:8). After baptism we strive with all our might to live in such a way as to merit the companionship of the Holy Ghost. But the Spirit is not something that may be programmed, plotted out, manufactured, or elicited; the influences of the Holy Ghost certainly cannot be demanded or coerced. We cannot force spiritual things, nor should a speaker cavalierly announce that the congregation is "about to have a spiritual experience." The Prophet Joseph Smith taught that "a man may receive the Holy Ghost, and it may descend upon him and not tarry with him" (D&C 130:23).

We know that the Spirit will not dwell with those who are unclean and thus are unworthy of its companionship (1 Corinthians 3:16–17; 6:19; compare 1 Nephi 10:21; 15:34; Alma 7:21; 3 Nephi 27:19). In addition, we cannot always tell when we will be filled with the Spirit and when we will not. Worthiness is only one variable. We may end the day on fire with the power of the Spirit, rejoicing in our blessings, grateful for the closeness we have felt to the Lord. When we arise a few short hours later, it would not be uncommon to feel as though we had lost something, to feel that the distance between us and Deity had increased dramatically. We ask ourselves search-ingly: "What happened? Did I sin during the night? Did I do something to change what I was feeling but a short time ago?" As it is in the temporal world, so it is in the spiritual world: we can study and pray and fast and strive to live worthy of the guiding and sanctifying influence of the Holy Ghost, but we cannot force spiritual things. This is another area over which we do not have complete control.

I knew one man who claimed that he would be perfect by the age of thirty. He set out on a deliberate program, organized his goals according to a ten-year, five-year, one-year, monthly, weekly, and daily plan. He pushed and pulled and stretched and reached spiritually, as much as any person I have known. But he was not perfect at thirty. You cannot force spiritual things. I am acquainted with a woman who announced to several of our friends that she would make her calling and elec-tion sure by the time she was fifty years old. She has been faith-ful in the Church. She has long since passed the age of fifty and is terribly discouraged because the goal of her existence, so far as she knows, has not been realized. You cannot force spiritual things.

Endless prayers, lengthy scripture vigils, excessive fasting—all of these, though at first well-intended, may come to be more a curse than a blessing. Gospel growth must come slowly, steadily, gradually. In that same spirit, we ought to be careful about setting goals for ourselves or others in areas over which we have limited control. Elder Boyd K. Packer has warned: "Such words as *compel, coerce, constrain, pressure, demand* do not describe our privileges with the Spirit.

"You can no more force the Spirit to respond than you can force a bean to sprout, or an egg to hatch before its time. You can create a climate to foster growth; you can nourish, and protect; but you cannot force or compel: You must await the growth.

"Do not be impatient to gain great spiritual knowledge. Let it grow, help it grow; but do not force it, or you will open the way to be misled."[1]

Our present must not be held hostage by the mistakes or *misdeeds of the past*. One wonders just how frustrated and soul-sick Saul of Tarsus and Alma and the sons of Mosiah must have been as they sought diligently—with a zeal known only to those who have been reborn from darkness to light—to repair the wrongs of their past. These men had gone about to destroy the church of God, had proven a major stumbling block to the progress of the kingdom of God. Then they had been stopped in their tracks, turned about, and redirected in their zeal. They did their best to make things right but in the end had to leave it all with God and move on.

The past is gone. The future is not here yet, and so it doesn't belong to us. All that we have is now. We cannot afford to live our lives in the past, to waste away our hours in fond reflection of simpler times or when things were much less complicated. Nor can we allow our anticipation of a brighter day to becloud our present and make ineffective the limited time we have here. In short, although many, many aspects of life are out of our control, there are things we *can* do to change the world and, perhaps more important, to change ourselves. For example:

1. *We can learn to adapt to change in a "living Church."* In the preface to the revelations in the Doctrine and Covenants, the Lord speaks of "the only true and living church upon the face of the whole earth, with which I, the Lord, am well

pleased" (D&C 1:30). Elder Neal A. Maxwell has observed that "when the word *living* is used, it carries a divinely deliberate connotation. The Church is neither dead nor dying, nor is it even wounded. The Church, like the living God who established it, is alive, aware, and functioning. It is not a museum that houses a fossilized faith; rather, it is a kinetic kingdom characterized by living faith in living disciples. . . .

"The living Church is one that responds to stimuli, that has movement, and that has the capacity to reproduce itself."[2]

"The doctrines will remain fixed, eternal," Elder Packer stated. "The organization, programs, and procedures will be altered as directed by Him whose church this is."[3] Policies change. Procedures change. Auxiliaries change. Calls come and releases come, and men and women of differing capacity and varied strengths and aptitudes serve for a season and then are called to serve elsewhere. Tragically, too many gifted men who were closely associated with Joseph Smith and had a place at his side in the very beginning of this dispensation could not adapt to change. As Church membership grew and as the organization of the restored Church began to unfold line upon line, precept upon precept, they simply could not deal with the fact that a living God in heaven, operating through a living tree of life on earth, could and would make alterations in his inspired kingdom.

2. *We can learn to say to God, "Thy will be done," and mean it.* This is tough. It's hard not to be in control of things. But one of the lessons of life that is beginning to dawn on me as I find myself closer to the casket than the cradle is this: God really is involved in the detail of our lives. He really cares. And he knows us—our needs, our challenges, our points of weakness, our strengths—far better than we know ourselves. He can

thus do far more to make our lives positive and productive—if we let him, for we can prevent him if we choose—than we could ever do. That is why it's just plain smart to learn to yield our hearts to him (Helaman 3:35). The promise in scripture is that if we have an eye single to the glory of God he will fill us with light and empower us to see everything more clearly (D&C 88:67–68).

It is true that praying "Thy will be done" may entail submitting to difficult or challenging circumstances ahead. C. S. Lewis provides a slightly different approach to this scripture: "'Thy will *be done*.' But a great deal of it is to be done by God's creatures; including me. The petition, then, is not merely that I may patiently suffer God's will but also that I may vigorously do it. I must be an agent as well as a patient. I am asking that I may be enabled to do it. . . .

"Taken this way, I find the words have a more regular daily application. For there isn't always—or we don't always have reason to suspect that there is—some great affliction looming in the near future, but there are always duties to be done; usually, for me, neglected duties to be caught up with. 'Thy will be *done*—by me—now' brings one back to brass tacks." Further, Lewis explained, "Thy will be done" may also imply a readiness on our part to receive and experience new and unanticipated blessings. "I know it sounds fantastic," he added, "but think it over. It seems to me that we often, almost sulkily, reject the good that God offers us because, at that moment, we expected some other good."[4] "Thy will be done" thus represents our petition that the Almighty work his wonders through us, that he soften our hearts to new ideas and new avenues of understanding, and that he open us to new paths and new doors of opportunity when it is best for us to move in another direction.

3. *We can learn to rely more upon our infinite and incomparable Redeemer.* Though such matters as self-reliance and self-confidence may prove to be valuable in some of our dealings in this life, the reciprocal principles of submission, surrender, and having an eye single to the glory of God are essential if we are to acquire that enabling power described in scripture as the saving grace of Jesus Christ. It is as if the Lord inquires of us: "Do you want to be a possessor of all things so that all things are subject unto you?" We, of course, respond in the affirmative. He then says: "Good. Then submit to me. Yield your heart unto me." The Lord asks further: "Do you want to have victory over all things?" We nod. He follows up: "Then surrender to me. Unconditionally." Odd, isn't it? We incorporate the great powers of divinity into ourselves only through acknowledging our own inabilities, accepting our limitations, and realizing our weakness. We open ourselves to infinite strength only through accepting our finite condition. We in time gain control through being willing to relinquish control.

I am haunted by the words Paul wrote in his second epistle to the Corinthians. As you know, Paul was, sadly, required to spend a significant amount of time defending his apostolic calling. Having been a zealous Pharisee and even a persecutor of the Christians before his conversion, and not having been one of the original witnesses of the resurrection of Christ, he felt the need to testify to his detractors that his call had indeed come from God. In doing so with the Corinthian Saints, he went on to describe some of the marvelous spiritual experiences the Lord had given to him. "And lest I should be exalted above measure," Paul hastened to add, "through the abundance of the revelations, there was given to me a thorn in the flesh, the messenger of Satan to buffet me, lest I should be exalted above measure. For this thing I besought the Lord thrice, that it might depart from me. And [the Lord] said unto me, My *grace is sufficient for thee: for my strength is made perfect in weakness.*" Paul then remarks: "Most gladly therefore will I rather glory in my infirmities, that the power of Christ may rest upon me. Therefore I take pleasure in infirmities, in reproaches, in necessities, in persecutions, in distresses for Christ's sake: for *when I am weak, then am I strong*" (2 Corinthians 12:7–10; emphasis added).

No one really knows what Paul's "thorn in the flesh" was. Was it a lingering sickness, perhaps malaria, so common in Galatia? Was it a memory of his past, a hellish reminder of who he had been? Was it an evil spirit that dogged his steps and wearied him in his ministry? Perhaps one day we'll know. All we know for sure is that whatever it was, it kept Paul humble and forced him to his knees. His inabilities and his impotence in the face of this particular challenge were ever before him. I rather think that when Paul states that he "besought the Lord thrice" for the removal of the thorn that he is not describing merely three prayers but instead three seasons of prayer, extended periods of wrestling and laboring in the Spirit for a specific blessing that never came. Indeed, as he suggests, another kind of blessing came—a closeness, a sensitivity, an acquaintance with Deity, a sanctified strength that came through pain and suffering. It was up against the wall of faith, when shorn of self-assurance and naked in his extremity and his frightening finitude, that a mere mortal received that enabling power we know as the grace of Christ. As the Savior explained to Moroni, when we acknowledge and confess our weakness—not just our specific weaknesses, our individual sins, but our weakness, our mortal limitation—and submit unto him, he will transform our weakness into strength (Ether 12:27).

We all have times in our lives, painful times when we have broken something, spiritually speaking, which we cannot repair. President Packer explained that "sometimes you *cannot* give back what you have taken because you don't have it to give. If you have caused others to suffer unbearably—defiled someone's virtue, for example—it is not within your power to give it back. . . .

". . . If you cannot undo what you have done, you are trapped. It is easy to understand how helpless and hopeless you then feel and why you might want to give up, just as Alma did.

"The thought that rescued Alma, when he acted upon it, is this: Restoring what you cannot restore, healing the wound you cannot heal, fixing that which you broke and you cannot fix is the very purpose of the atonement of Christ.

"When your desire is firm and you are willing to pay the 'uttermost farthing' (Matthew 5:25–26), the law of restitution is suspended. Your obligation is transferred to the Lord. He will settle your accounts."[5]

4. *We can learn to "wait on the Lord."* One of my favorite scriptures comes from Paul's first letter to the Corinthians. Paul acknowledged to the Saints in Corinth that when he visited them he "came not with excellency of speech or of wisdom" but rather he "determined not to know any thing among [them], save Jesus Christ, and him crucified." In sweet humility this learned and impressive orator then added this treasure: "But as it is written, Eye hath not seen, nor ear heard, neither

have entered into the heart of man, the things which God hath prepared for them that love him" (1 Corinthians 2:1–2, 9).

That expression is a comforting assurance to each and every one of us, a reminder that while there are moments of intense joy and peace in this world, the glories and feelings and transcendent associations of a future world are even grander. As powerful and encouraging as these thoughts are, they are not Paul's property alone: they were spoken first by Isaiah, and, incidentally, in a slightly different manner. "For since the beginning of the world," Isaiah declared, "men have not heard, nor perceived by the ear, neither hath the eye seen, O God, beside thee, what he hath prepared *for him that waiteth for him*" (Isaiah 64:4; emphasis added; compare D&C 133:45).

To wait on the Lord is closely related to having *hope* in the Lord. Waiting on and hoping in the Lord are scriptural words that focus not on frail and faltering mortals but rather on a sovereign and omni-loving God who fulfills his promises to the people of promise in his own time.

Hope is more than worldly wishing. It is expectation, anticipation, assurance. We wait on the Lord because we have hope in him. "For we through the Spirit wait for the hope of righteousness by faith" (Galatians 5:5). Thus, we wait on the Lord—not in the sense that we sit and wring our hands and glance at our clocks periodically, but rather that we exercise patience in his providential hand, knowing full well, by the power of the Holy Ghost, that the Father of Lights will soon transform a darkened world, all in preparation for the personal ministry of the Light of the World (1 Corinthians 1:4–8).

To be impatient with God is to lose sight of the fact— and thus require regular reminders—that our Heavenly Father loves us, is mindful of our present problems and daily dilemmas, and has a plan, both cosmic and personal, for our happiness here and our eternal reward hereafter. To wait on him, on the other hand, is to be "confident of this very thing, that he which hath begun a good work in you will perform it until the day of [the coming of] Jesus Christ" (Philippians 1:6). That is, to wait on the Lord is to exercise a lively hope that the God who is in his heaven is also working upon and through his people on earth. As it was anciently, so it is in our day: the spiritual regeneration required of individuals and whole societies that results in the establishment of Zion takes place "in process of time" (Moses 7:21). Elder Neal A. Maxwell declared that "since the Lord wants a people 'tried in all things' (D&C 136:31), how, specifically, will we be tried? He tells us, I will try the faith and the patience of my people (see Mosiah 23:21). Since faith in the timing of the Lord may be tried, let us learn to say not only, 'Thy will be done,' but patiently also, 'Thy timing be done.'"[6]

It is especially difficult to witness the seeming prosperity of the perverse, as wickedness widens and malevolence multiplies. But the scriptural counsel is to "rest in the Lord, and wait patiently for him: fret not thyself because of him who prospereth in his way, because of the man who bringeth wicked devices to pass" (Psalms 37:7). Or, "Say not thou, I will recompense evil; but wait on the Lord, and he shall save thee" (Proverbs 20:22). Indeed, the glorious assurance, particularly to those of us who live in the midst of crime and indecency, is: "Hast thou not known? hast thou not heard, that *the everlasting God, the Lord, the Creator of the ends of the earth, fainteth not, neither is weary? there is no searching of his understanding. He giveth power to the faint; and to them that have no might he increaseth strength.* Even the youths shall faint and be weary, and the young men shall utterly fall: But *they that wait upon the Lord shall renew their strength;* they shall mount up with wings as eagles; they shall run, and not be weary; and they shall walk, and not faint" (Isaiah 40:28–31; emphasis added).

There are certain constants in a world of change, constants on which we can lean in desperate moments. For example:

God lives, as does his Beloved Son, the risen Redeemer.

We are the spirit children of God, his sons and daughters, and we have limitless possibilities and unlimited potential to do good and accomplish his purposes.

God has a plan, a plan of salvation that provides meaning and purpose to our existence.

Jesus Christ is the divine Son of God, our Savior and Redeemer, who came to earth to suffer and bleed and die and rise again from the tomb, to atone for the sins of all human-kind.

There are absolute truths and absolute values, rights and wrongs that transcend custom or social consensus.

The Church of Jesus Christ, together with its doctrines and priesthoods, has been restored and reestablished once again on earth.

We are here to gain experience, to develop and enhance valued relationships, and to prepare our souls for what lies ahead.

The family is the most important unit in time and in eternity. The perpetuation of that family into eternity is a vital part of eternal life, the greatest of all the gifts of God (D&C 14:7).

When we die, we do not cease to be; we merely cease to be in this sphere. Life continues after the transition we know as death. Through Jesus Christ our Lord, we have hope in the immortality of the soul and the inseparable union of body and spirit.

We could go on and on, but the above list seems sufficient to remind us that in a world that is too often built on shifting sand, there are truths and certainties and absolutes that we may depend upon with great confidence. In my own life, I have found especial comfort in knowing of and turning to the cleansing and enabling power of Jesus Christ. At those times when I have been in the greatest agony, I have found myself reflecting on and even echoing the words of Alma as he faced the challenge of proselytizing among the Zoramites: "O Lord, wilt thou give me strength, that I may bear with mine infirmities. For I am infirm, and such wickedness among this people doth pain my soul. O Lord, my heart is exceedingly sorrowful; wilt thou comfort my soul in Christ" (Alma 31:30–31). Truly, as Paul exulted, "I can do all things through Christ [who] strengtheneth me" (Philippians 4:13; compare Alma 26:12).

"It is as demonstrated in Christ," Elder Jeffrey R. Holland taught, "that 'charity never faileth.' It is that charity—his pure love for us—without which we would be nothing, hopeless, of all men and women most miserable. Truly, those found possessed of the blessings of his love at the last day—the Atonement, the Resurrection, eternal life, eternal promise— surely it shall be well with them." In short, "Life has its share of fears and failures. Sometimes things fall short. Sometimes people fail us, or economies or businesses or governments fail us. But one thing in time or eternity does *not* fail us—the pure love of Christ."[7]

Just as we must not allow the few unsettled questions in life to blind us to the almost limitless number of answers to be found in the restored gospel, so we must not permit the things out of our control to control us, to cause us to slip or stumble. There is an inner peace and a quiet strength that flow into the lives of those who lean upon and trust in those truths we know for sure, those matters upon which we can rely with undeterred certainty. God is in control, and that's enough for me.

NOTES

1. *That All May Be Edified*; 338; emphasis in original.

2. *Things As They Really Are*, 46; emphasis in original.

3. Conference Report, October 1989, 19.

4. *Letters to Malcolm: Chiefly on Prayer*, 25–26.

5. Conference Report, October 1995, 23; emphasis in original.

6. Conference Report, April 2001, 76.

7. *Christ and the New Covenant*, 336, 337.

9

TAKING NO THOUGHT—
OR PLANNING AHEAD?

D uring the early 1970s there was much anxiety among the people in the United States, both within and without the Church, concerning the economy and the state of the nation. The Vietnam War had taken not only many thousands of lives but also a major emotional toll on the American people. In addition, we had just passed through the trauma of Watergate, and confidence in government and governmental officials was at an all-time low. Many self-proclaimed prophets of doom published books, delivered lectures, and frequented talk shows to discuss the decline and fall of the American economy.

Unfortunately, members of the Church were not immune to the effects of such sensationalism. I remember encountering many Latter-day Saints who spoke often of the demise of the United States, an imminent overthrow of America by the communists, the collapse of the economy, and the impending Second Coming. College students dropped out of school. Many young couples decided to let their insurance premiums lapse. Others chose not to buy a home. Why such reactions? Because, they said, the end is near, the coming crisis is upon us. Why waste money or effort when it's all going to be over any day now? It was a pretty scary time.

Well, as you may have noticed, the nation didn't dissolve, the economy didn't collapse, and the Millennium did not begin. The leaders of the Church have assured us that while we are certainly closer to the end of time than ever before, there is much to do, much to experience, and much to accomplish before the Lord Jesus comes to dwell on this earth. There is a need to live on, to live providently, to live productively, to live with an eye to the future. We must plan ahead. The wisest among us set money aside for savings and advanced schooling or training, have a year's supply of food, position ourselves to be able to serve missions in the years ahead, and develop a strategy for retirement and our advanced years.

Those who lived in a bygone day said it like this: "I know the Lord will come before too very long, but I still plant cherry trees." That is, we have been counseled to live in the present, to appreciate and enjoy all that is virtuous, lovely, and of good report in our day. We have been advised to live today as though the future is well ahead of us—to set reasonable goals for ourselves, to purchase and build homes, to buy insurance, and, in general, to do some long-range planning.

I believe the key is for us to strike a balance. Though those who do not think about the future at all seldom arrive there in a state of preparation, though there is much to recommend about time management and goal-setting programs (in terms of making maximum use of our time and resources), there is another side to the story. While we should look to the future, plan for the future, and anticipate living in the future, we must not become obsessed with the future. We are called upon to live *now*. The Savior, in his Sermon on the Mount, instructed us to "take no thought for your life, what ye shall eat, or what ye shall drink; nor yet for your body, what ye shall put on. Is not the life more than meat, and the body than raiment?" He added: "Take therefore no thought for the morrow: for the morrow shall take thought for the things of itself" (Matthew 6:25, 34). In studying this passage, let's keep a few things in mind. First of all, these words were delivered primarily to the Twelve, to those who would go into the world without purse or scrip as full-time ministers of the gospel. Second, "take no thought" doesn't really mean "don't think about" but rather "don't be overly anxious about" or "don't fret and worry about." The Lord's counsel to his disciples is to avoid being fixated on or riveted to the future.

The Lutheran theologian Dietrich Bonhoeffer commented on the Master's words as follows: "Be not anxious! Earthly possessions dazzle our eyes and delude us into thinking that they can provide security and freedom from anxiety. Yet all the time they are the very source of all anxiety. If our hearts are set on them, our reward is an anxiety whose burden is intolerable. Anxiety creates its own treasures and they in turn beget further care. When we seek for security in possessions, we are trying to drive out care with care, and the net result is the precise opposite of our anticipations. The fetters which bind us to our possessions prove to be cares themselves.

"The way to misuse our possessions is to use them as an insurance against the morrow. Anxiety is always directed to the morrow, whereas goods are in the strictest sense meant to be used only for to-day. By trying to ensure for the next day we are only creating uncertainty today. . . . The only way to win assurance is by leaving to-morrow entirely in the hands of God and by receiving from him all we need for to-day."[1]

Let's not misunderstand Bonhoeffer. It isn't that we shouldn't plan ahead or save or even put things in store. It is that the Lord does not want us to become so enamored with our future holdings that they in fact hold us hostage; in short, we must not be possessed by our possessions, either here and now or thirty years from now. Thus, the man or woman who, like Scrooge McDuck, spends every waking moment focused on making money, acquiring more and more property, and building an inexhaustible supply of toys for the future—all to the exclusion of the weightier matters of life—is in reality mining fool's gold. Such a one will learn the harsh realities concerning "slippery riches" (Helaman 13:31) one day to his own cost and loss. "For where your treasure is, there will your heart be also" (Matthew 6:21).

I have also witnessed a related phenomenon that is really quite sad. Sometimes persons who are overly tied to their goals or regimented in their plan do not allow themselves to be open to appropriate interruption. They tend to view people and people's problems or questions as distractions or hindrances, as objects which move them off course. In the same way, those who have planned all their life for A, are doing everything in their power to pursue A, and become obsessed with that great end are occasionally oblivious or insensitive to small promptings, slight impressions from on high to respond to a newly opened door.

On a number of occasions I have been asked by young students to describe the path that brought me to my present profession. I have usually stated that my path has been anything but a simple and straight one. After I had finished a master's degree, I was accepted into a doctoral program. I was loving my course work, was stimulated by my role as a graduate instructor, and fully expected to be working as a clinical psychologist in three or four years. I reflected occasionally upon the future but never really worried about much beyond the next week's reading or writing assignments. I had heard fellow clinical psychology students refer occasionally to an organization called LDS Social Services, but I really knew nothing about it. One day I was sitting at a desk reading when the thought weighed upon me that I should contact LDS Social Services and find out about their various programs. And so on the basis of an ever so slight urging from on high, I called and made an appointment.

I drove to Salt Lake City a few days later and visited the agency. My intention was to speak for a moment with a worker and then perhaps get some literature describing their work. But I soon learned that the people there thought I was there for another reason. I was introduced to a very kindly gentleman who introduced himself to me and asked me to be seated in his office. We chatted informally for about thirty minutes about Brigham Young University, the behavioral sciences, and the answers to age-old questions that come to us through the restored gospel. There was an unusual spirit in the room, a peaceful feeling, a sense that what was being said needed to be said. The man then told me all about LDS Social Services and surprised me with the question: "Now, Brother Millet, which of those programs would you be most interested in working in?"

I thought to myself: "Bless his heart. He thinks I'm here for a job. I just came to get a brochure! But I don't want to hurt his feelings. I'll go along with this for a while." And so I answered his question and explained which of their programs appealed to me the most.

He nodded and said, "That's what I thought."

His next question truly startled me. "Brother Millet, would you be willing to go anywhere in the country to work?"

Again, I thought, "My goodness, he is really pursuing this matter. I'll go one more step before I pop the balloon."

I answered, "Yes, I suppose I would."

He then asked, "How does Idaho Falls sound to you?"

I found myself saying, "Sounds good."

He paused for a moment, and I sat silently wondering where this was really going. Then he said, "Brother Millet, that stack of papers on my desk is a pile of applications from people who would like very much to work for LDS Social Services. But I'm offering you a job right now if you'll take it."

It's hard to verbalize what I then felt. There was the strange irony of the moment, the odd and almost humorous realization that the man behind that desk and I had entered the interview with two different intentions. But there was also a feeling that I knew very well, one I had come to know over the years—the feeling that we were being moved along by an unseen power, the quiet nudge of the Spirit, to enter a new door that was now opening. Without hesitation I responded: "I'll take it."

I spent the next forty-five minutes on the way home trying to organize my thoughts and prepare a nice way to say to my sweetheart: "Okay, pack up the tent. We're moving on." In addition, I needed to find a way to become disengaged from my schooling and assignments at the university as gracefully as I could. As difficult as the latter challenge was for me (including bruising some feelings here and there of those to whom I had made commitments), I knew what needed to be done. My conversation with Shauna was, in fact, a very moving experience. I walked into the apartment, she inquired how my day had gone, and I asked her to sit and visit with me for a moment. I said: "Brace yourself. I have something to tell you." I then rehearsed the episode in Salt Lake City and, thankfully, felt the same Spirit come into the room that I had enjoyed an hour earlier.

Shauna responded, with tears in her eyes, "We're supposed to do this, aren't we?" I nodded.

Similar things have happened in regard to major professional decisions again and again during our thirty-plus years of marriage. Don't get me wrong: I don't think we are a flaky couple, tossed to and fro by every whim and thought that make their way into our minds. We have tried to live a sane and balanced life, to be prayerful, diligent, and dependable. We have prayed earnestly for divine direction in all phases of our lives, and we feel we have been attentive and receptive when God has spoken. I would not, however, be speaking the truth if I were to suggest to you that I have always known exactly what course my professional life would take. I have not. But we have loved our lives. Our brief time with LDS Social Services was life changing, and some of the friendships we developed and lessons we learned in Idaho will be with us all our days. And then another door opened, and we entered. A few years later another one opened, and, once again, we walked through.

We live in difficult times, and there are days now (and there will surely be more challenging ones in the future) when we may be tempted to close up the shop of everyday life and look with despair upon the future. We must not yield to such temptations. To turn an expression of the Prophet Joseph to a different context, "There is much which lieth in futurity, pertaining to the saints" (D&C 123:15). And so we look ahead, plan for the future, and begin now putting things in their

proper order. We are neither ignorant nor naïve about the tests
and trials ahead, but we will not yield ourselves to the spirit of
cynicism. And so we look to the future, but we are not captivated or ensnared with anxiety regarding the future. We set
goals but are open to a change in plans, knowing full well that
He who notices the fall of the sparrow is conscious of and will
lead his chosen people along the pathways of life.

NOTE

1. *The Cost of Discipleship*, 197–98.

10

STANDING IN HOLY PLACES

The Savior soberly spoke of an "overflowing scourge" and a "desolating sickness" that will grip the land in the last days. The Lord then added a prophetic insight that is simple but comforting: "But my disciples shall stand in holy places, and shall not be moved" (D&C 45:31–32). There is safety in holiness, security in standing in holy places. The children sing it: "Keep the commandments; keep the commandments! In this there is safety; in this there is peace."[1]

And what are the holy places in which we are to stand? They are the temples, the church houses, the homes of the Latter-day Saints. We are to become, first of all, a temple-centered people, a body of believers who are covenant conscious and focused on the things of eternity. Bearing in our souls "the testimony of the covenant" (D&C 109:38), we strive to make the temple, as President Howard W. Hunter counseled us, the great symbol of our Church membership.[2]

In that same spirit, we devote ourselves to faithful attendance and enthusiastic participation in the programs of the Church. This is the Lord's Church, and he is at the head of it. Through the principles, ordinances, teachings, and organized sacrifice provided by the Church, we purify our hearts, come to love and cherish one another, and mature in our relationship to God. We need the Church and feel undying gratitude for its restoration in these last days.

We go to church and to the temple to enter into sacred covenants, and we come home to keep those covenants and to live and practice the precepts we have been taught. The home is the most sacred of all institutions in the kingdom of God, for it houses the family—the most important unit in time and in eternity. We learn to be reverent and attentive to spiritual things in the temple and the church, but we apply these timeless lessons in the home. President David O. McKay thus taught that "a home in which unity, mutual helpfulness, and love abide is just a bit of heaven on earth."[3]

While the temple, the church house, and the home are and should be holy places, there is another holy place that in some ways is even more important to us. I speak of where we are, spiritually speaking, at any given time. For surely it is not where we are living or what ward we are attending that matters most; is it *how* we are living. And to the degree that we are living the gospel, doing our very best to keep our covenants, the Spirit of the Lord will be with us; where that Spirit is, there is peace and liberty and security. Therein is a holy place. "For I am able to make you holy," the Savior said, "and your sins are forgiven you" (D&C 60:7). That peace and safety can come to us in Paramus, New Jersey, or Portland, Oregon. It can come to us in Saganaw, Michigan, as well as in Salt Lake City, Utah. The peaceful assurance that the Lord is in our midst (D&C 38:7) and is guarding his flock can come to the smallest branch of the Church, as well as the largest Latter-day Saint stronghold.

There is a myth that continues to sweep the Church to the

effect that one day all of the Saints will gather physically to Independence, Missouri, or to Salt Lake City. One problem with this thought is that it violates the principle set forth by Isaiah the prophet, who spoke of expanding the tent of Zion by driving more and more tent pegs (stakes) into the ground (Isaiah 54:2; compare 33:20). Growth and expansion in the kingdom do not occur as everyone comes into the center of the tent, as it were, but rather as more and more stakes are grounded, and the walls of the tent thereby expand to take in more and more people. "For Zion must increase in beauty, and in holiness; her borders must be enlarged; her stakes must be strengthened; yea, verily I say unto you, Zion must arise and put on her beautiful garments" (D&C 82:14).[4]

"There will be here and there a Stake [of Zion] for the gathering of the Saints," Joseph Smith taught. "Some may have cried peace, but the Saints and the world will have little peace from henceforth. Let this not hinder us from going to the Stakes. . . . There your children shall be blessed, and you in the midst of friends . . . may be blessed."[5]

Elder Harold B. Lee spoke during World War II of the need to stand in holy places. "I know now that the place of safety in this world is not in any given place; *it doesn't make so much difference where we live; but the all-important thing is how we live, and I have found that the security can come to Israel only when they keep the commandments,* when they live so that they can enjoy the companionship, the direction, the comfort, and the guidance of the Holy Spirit of the Lord, *when they are willing to listen to these men whom God has set here to preside as His mouthpieces,* and when we obey the counsels of the Church."[6]

Our hope is in Christ. Our hope is not and cannot rest solely on mortal men and women, no matter how good or noble they may be. Hope is more than wishing, more than yearning for some eventuality or some possession. Gospel hope is a solid and sure conviction. Hope is expectation. Anticipation. Assurance. The Saints of the Most High—those who have come out of the world, put off the natural man, and put on Christ—these are they who are entitled to "a more excellent hope" (Ether 12:32). Hope flows from faith, faith in the Lord Jesus Christ. When we have faith in him, we believe in him—who he is and what he has done. Further, we believe he can do what he says he can do—make us clean and whole; make us pure before God the Father; make us happy, productive, and contributing members of his grand kingdom. Mormon taught: "And again, my beloved brethren [and sisters], I would speak unto you concerning hope. How is it that ye can attain unto faith, save ye shall [then] have hope? And what is it that ye shall hope for? Behold I say unto you that *ye shall have hope through the atonement of Christ and the power of his resurrection, to be raised unto life eternal,* and this because of your faith in him according to the promise" (Moroni 7:40–41; emphasis added; compare Ether 12:4).

And what is our indication that we are on course? How do we know we are standing in holy places? "Hereby know we that we dwell in him, and he in us, because he hath given us of his Spirit" (1 John 4:13). The presence of God's Spirit is the attestation, the divine assurance that we are headed in the right direction. It is God's seal, his anointing, his unction (1 John 2:20) to us that our lives are in order.

I can still recall very vividly the fear and awful anxiety that my wife, Shauna, and I felt when we decided to purchase our first home. We had no money in savings, and though I had a steady job it did not bring a hefty income. Yet we knew we had to get started some time if we ever hoped to become home-owners. We determined to start slowly. A dear friend of ours, a fellow seminary teacher, located a place for us in his neighborhood. Another seminary teacher friend offered to loan us the down payment. (Thank goodness for friends!) It was at this time that Shauna and I became acquainted with the concept of "earnest money." We made a goodwill payment to the owner of the home, a small amount to be sure, but an amount that was sufficient to evidence our seriousness about purchasing the place. That amount was called the earnest money. It was a token payment, a gesture of our desire to acquire a home, a promise of our intent.

God works with us in similar ways. How can he communicate to us that we are following a proper course? As we indicated above, he can send his Spirit. The Holy Ghost thus represents God's "earnest money" on us, his down payment, his goodwill gesture and assurance to us that he is serious about saving us, and that one day he will own us and claim us fully as his. Indeed, the same Spirit that eventually seals us up unto eternal life places a seal of approval upon our lives here and now (2 Corinthians 1:21–22; 5:5; Ephesians 1:13–14). Though the fulness of the blessings of eternal life are not available until the world to come, the peace and rest and hope that are harbingers of those unspeakable blessings can and should be ours in this world.

We cannot overcome the world if we are worldly. We cannot overcome the world if our trust is in the arm of flesh (2 Nephi 4:34). And we cannot overcome the world if we live in a constant state of spiritual insecurity. Satan, the arch-deceiver, is versatile and observant. As surely as the day follows the night, he will strike at our sense of insecurity before God if we do not acquire that hope or assurance that comes by and through His Holy Spirit. We overcome the world through Christ—through being changed by Christ, captained by Christ, and consumed in Christ.[7] During the Last Supper, Jesus declared to his disciples: "These things I have spoken unto you, that in me ye might have peace. In the world ye shall have tribulation: but be of good cheer; I have overcome the world" (John 16:33).

To what extent, then, are we prepared to meet God? How ready are we to enter into heavenly places and to sit among glorified beings? Few of us would dare rush forward and volunteer to sign the list of names of the sanctified. But the revelations of God and the teachings of his servants affirm that if we are faithful in the Church, worthy of participation in the holy temple, and enjoying the fruits and benefits of the Holy Spirit—to that degree we are prepared to meet God.

"Where is there safety in the world today?" President Harold B. Lee asked. "Safety can't be won by tanks and guns and the airplanes and atomic bombs. There is only one place of safety and that is within the realm of the power of Almighty God that he gives to those who keep his commandments and listen to his voice, as he speaks through the channels that he has ordained for that purpose."[8]

We do not need to be possessed of an unholy or intemperate zeal in order to be saved; we need to be constant and dependable. God is the other party with us in the gospel covenant. He is the controlling partner. He lets us know, through the influence of the Holy Ghost, that the gospel covenant is still intact and the supernal promises are sure. The Savior invites us to learn the timeless and comforting lesson that "he who doeth the works of righteousness shall receive his reward, even peace in this world, and eternal life in the world to come" (D&C 59:23). Peace. Hope. Assurance. Security. These things come to us by virtue of the atoning blood of Jesus Christ and as a natural result of our wholehearted efforts to stand in holy places.

NOTES

    1. Barbara A. McConochie, "Keep the Commandments," in *Hymns of The Church of Jesus Christ of Latter-day Saints*, no. 303.

    2. Conference Report, October 1994, 8.

    3. *Gospel Ideals*, 477–78.

    4. See Bruce R. McConkie, *The Millennial Messiah*, 294–96.

    5. *Teachings of the Prophet Joseph Smith*, 160.

    6. Conference Report, April 1943, 129; emphasis added.

    7. See Ezra Taft Benson, Conference Report, October 1985, 5–6.

    8. Conference Report, October 1973, 169.

11

ROOTED, GROUNDED, ESTABLISHED

A number of years ago a particular book was sweeping the country and eliciting special interest among Latter-day Saints. Though it was written by a Latter-day Saint, it was released by a national publishing house, and thus its popularity and its sales swelled. Within about a year after its release, it was not uncommon to hear the book discussed in priesthood and Relief Society meetings, sacrament meetings, and youth firesides. I even heard of a stake president recommending, in the main session of stake conference, that members of the stake acquire the book and study it carefully.

While I'm a real sucker for new books, for some reason I was a bit slow about buying a copy of this book and even slower about reading it. I remember finally sitting down and beginning my reading and study in earnest. I was not very far into the work before I began to be troubled with what I found. Though the story line was fascinating and the details made for interesting consideration, the doctrinal messages, shallow and disguised as they were for those of other faiths, were off target; I began, in fact, to make notes of the problematic parts of the book. I took my rather unofficial review and filed it away.

Early one Saturday morning a few weeks later, I received a

phone call from one of the General Authorities of the Church. After I recovered a bit from the call itself and after we had spent a few moments in light chatter, the Church leader asked, "Bob, have you read the book by _____?" I indicated that I had read the book. He asked me what I thought of it.

"Well, it's a fascinating story. I can see why people around the country, including Latter-day Saints, are quite taken by the book. It's intriguing."

"Any other impressions?" he asked.

I was hesitant to say anything too negative and so I added the quip: "I just wish my books sold like this book!"

"Anything further?" he persisted.

I finally responded, "There are some things about the book that make me very nervous."

"Well, I hope so," he followed up. "What are they?" I then began to recite what I considered to be the doctrinal flaws of the book, expressing with each item where I felt the book was at odds with principles of truth that have been set forth in the standard works or revealed through modern apostles and prophets. The words that followed are indelibly impressed upon my soul. He said: "It never ceases to amaze me how gullible the Latter-day Saints can be when it comes to printed material like this. Our lack of doctrinal depth and gospel understanding in general makes many of us an easy prey to every passing craze."

We need to be solid, void of sensationalism, and rooted in restored truth if we are to face squarely the challenges of our day and engage with courage and conviction the demands of discipleship in a future day. That is to say, our own gospel scholarship needs to be steady and solid, focused on the principles and doctrines that matter most, and true to the teachings we have received in this dispensation. President Joseph Fielding Smith pointed out that "it makes no difference what is written or what anyone has said, if what has been said is in conflict with what the Lord has revealed, we can set it aside. My words, and the teachings of any other member of the Church, high or low, if they do not square with the revelations, we need not accept them. Let us have this matter clear. We have accepted the four standard works as the measuring yardsticks, or balances, by which we measure every man's doctrine."[1]

My colleagues and I receive phone calls, letters, and e-mails quite regularly from members of the Church throughout the world asking different gospel questions. Many of these are quite easy to handle, such as when the person simply needs a reference or source for something. Some of the letters I do not handle at all, inasmuch as they seem to describe the kinds of problems that ought to be dealt with by ecclesiastical authorities; these are forwarded to Church leaders. And then there is another category of questions: those that pertain to what I have come to call extraneous matters, tangential issues, areas of focus that are either so narrow or so abstract that it really doesn't matter. And I generally don't know the answer to their question anyway.

During the time that I served as dean of Religious Education at Brigham Young University, we often had inquiries from members of the Church about doctrine, Church history, or other religious areas. One week one of my associate deans and I had spent what seemed to be every available moment, Monday through Friday, dealing with unusual and strange requests, everything from anti-Mormon attacks to Latter-day Saints being proselytized to apostate cults. By Friday

afternoon at five o'clock I was absolutely exhausted. I was emotionally spent and mentally drained and commented to my
associate dean that over the weekend I might investigate the
possibility of starting a new career as a bricklayer or cattle
rancher!

At 5:15 P.M. the phone rang. A woman on the other end
of the line asked: "Brother Millet, do you have a moment for a
doctrinal question?" I sighed and said yes. She continued, "I've
been studying the book of Revelation this year and have come
upon some things that are confusing to me. For some time now
I have been in the thirteenth chapter and have been trying to
understand the details concerning the horns on the beast. Do
you have any recommendations?"

It really was a bad time to ask me that kind of question, for
no sooner had she ended the query than I fired back, "Yes, I
have a suggestion. Do you have something to write with?"

"I do," she said. "Go ahead."

I then said something that shouldn't have been said. "I recommend," I began with some gusto, "that you burn the book
of Revelation and read the Book of Mormon!"

There was, as you might suppose, a long pause. Then the
sister responded: "What was that again?" I repeated the
instruction exactly and with identical zeal. She reacted
timidly: "Oh, Brother Millet, you don't mean that, do you?
Don't you like the book of Revelation?"

I then said: "Sister _____, I'm sorry. It's been a long and
hard week. I shouldn't have said what I did. I love the
Apocalypse, and I believe it contains some of the greatest
encouragement and counsel we could receive in the last days,
especially as we confine ourselves to the grand, overarching
messages and not trip over the symbolic detail that has

not been explained by prophet leaders." I then added the following, somewhat cautiously: "One more thing. It seems to me that such a study could really prove a major spiritual distraction to you."

Again, a long pause, and then she spoke, this time with deep emotion. "Thank you, Brother Millet. I'm afraid you're right. I need to get back on course."

There is so much of beauty and depth and certainty and applicability within the covers of the standard works and the sermons of living prophets and apostles. Why would we even concern ourselves with flimsy matters, with tangential reading, when the mysteries of the kingdom of heaven are so readily available? Elder Bruce R. McConkie explained that "we are obligated to understand the basic doctrines which lead to eternal life; beyond this, how much we know about the mysteries depends upon the degree of our spiritual enlightenment. It is unwise to swim too far in water over our heads. (Mosiah 4:27; D&C 10:4.) My experience is that people who get themselves ensnared in fruitless contention over the meanings of deep and hidden passages of scripture are usually those who do not have a sound and basic understanding of the simple and basic truths of salvation."[2]

We are, to a large extent, a product of what we consume, whether that be in food or reading material. Thus, what we think about, how we perceive events in our own day, and to what degree we comprehend the scenes leading up to the second coming of the Son of Man will depend a great deal upon what we imbibe through serious study. There is a crying need for Latter-day Saints to be solid and secure in the faith, not just equipped with testimony and conviction but also fortified with a reason for the hope within them (1 Peter 3:15), with gospel understanding that is as satisfying to the mind as it is soothing to the heart. The apostle Paul counseled the Saints in his day: "As ye have therefore received Christ Jesus the Lord, so walk ye in him: rooted and built up in him, and stablished in the faith, as ye have been taught, abounding therein with thanksgiving" (Colossians 2:6–7). Our task, like that delivered to the former-day Saints, is to "continue in the faith grounded and settled, and be not moved away from the hope of the gospel" (Colossians 1:23). Spiritual stability comes from focusing on the fundamental verities of salvation and striving to align our hearts and minds with the word and will of God. Such a course leads to peace, to joy, to rest—to a settled conviction of the truth.

NOTES

1. *Doctrines of Salvation*, 3:203–4; emphasis removed.

2. *Doctrines of the Restoration*, 231–32.

12

WATCHMEN ON THE TOWER

I t is not uncommon to begin to teach the restored gospel to those not of our faith, to pray with and bear testimony to them, to respond to their questions, to even have them come to Church and meet the Saints, and then to have the investigator say something like this: "Look, elders (or sisters), I really appreciate all you are trying to do for me. I enjoy very much being with you and having you in my home. I have appreciated the chance to get to know some of the members in your local congregation and have been touched by the love in their families and their genuine commitment to their faith and way of life. The programs in your church for women, children, youth, and the care of the poor have fascinated and inspired me. I have been stimulated by many of the teachings of your church, especially the ones dealing with life before birth and life after death. The last few weeks have been very meaningful to me, and I have learned a great deal. But, to be completely honest with you, I just can't buy this stuff about Joseph Smith and visions and angels and gold plates. It's just a bit far-fetched. But I do like the other facets of your faith."

Such a statement is often baffling to the missionaries and downright perplexing to the members. This person, clearly touched by and impressed with the clean-cut, polite, and spiritually minded missionaries, as well as the deeply sincere Latter-day Saints in the local ward, is ready to accept one phase of Mormonism but reject the other. Specifically, he is prepared to accept the product of the revelation but unable or unwilling to accept the revelator. To put this another way, people are often eager to acknowledge the *fruits* of Mormonism—clean living, strong families, abiding faith in God—without similarly acknowledging the validity of the *roots* of Mormonism. If we could simply construct a religion which had our authority, doctrines, and practices, without at the same time linking ourselves to the First Vision or angelic ministrations, then surely more people would rush forward to be baptized.

But we cannot. Foundational doctrines and practices are built upon foundational events, namely, the appearance of God the Father and his Son Jesus Christ in the Sacred Grove in the spring of 1820, as well as a whole host of heavenly messengers, "all declaring their dispensation, their rights, their keys, their honors, their majesty and glory, and the power of their priesthood; giving line upon line, precept upon precept; here a little, and there a little; giving us consolation by holding forth that which is to come, confirming our hope!" (D&C 128:21). The Church of Jesus Christ of Latter-day Saints is "built upon the foundation of the apostles and prophets, Jesus Christ himself being the chief corner stone" (Ephesians 2:20). It is built upon the rock, the same rock upon which Jesus built his Church in the meridian of time (Matthew 16:13–19), the glorious rock of revelation.[1]

I have spent a good deal of time in the last decade interacting with men and women of other faiths. In some cases, I have developed deep and lasting friendships with these folks.

I am reminded of one gathering with a group made up of five Latter-day Saints and five Christians of another persuasion. We spent almost two days discussing the Latter-day Saint concept of Christ and the Atonement. We (the LDS contingent) responded to a myriad of questions, dispelled a multitude of myths about Mormonism, and read a few scriptures from the writings of Paul, but we spent a surprising amount of time reading and reflecting on the testimony of Book of Mormon prophets concerning the mercy and grace of the Savior.

The leader of the other group sat back in his chair and said, "This is impressive. I thought I understood all about you and your faith. I'm willing to put aside our differences on the Trinity, because few of us who accept it understand it. And for now I'm willing to set aside some of your beliefs and teachings about the nature of God. Do you know what we're left with, as far as major differences between us?"

I answered for the group: "What's that?"

He shot right back: "The First Vision and priesthood authority."

The five Latter-day Saints in the group looked at each other and smiled, and I said: "You're starting to understand us."

All that we teach and all that we believe is absolutely dependent upon our acceptance of the fact that there was a falling away, a lengthy season when divine authority and saving doctrines were lost from the earth; that God has called and empowered a modern prophet, Joseph Smith, to initiate what the scriptures call the "restitution of all things" (Acts 3:21); that the keys of power have continued in rightful succession from Joseph Smith to the senior apostles of God on earth, down to the present day; and that this Church of Jesus Christ of Latter-day Saints is in very deed the kingdom of God on earth and is preparing a people for the second coming of the Son of Man.

We sustain fifteen men as prophets, seers, and revelators. Their primary assignment is to serve as "special witnesses of the name of Christ in all the world" (D&C 107:23). They are *prophets*, inasmuch as "the testimony of Jesus is the spirit of prophecy" (Revelation 19:10). Further, as *revelators* they are charged by God to make known or reveal the will of God to the Church and to the world. They speak, as did their Master, as men having authority from God, and not as the learned of the day (JST Matthew 7:37). Finally, these chosen servants are called as *seers*, persons commissioned to see things afar off (D&C 101:54), things "not visible to the natural eye" (Moses 6:36). Ammon explained to Limhi that "a seer is a revelator and a prophet also; and a gift which is greater can no man have, except he should possess the power of God, which no man can; yet a man may have great power given him from God. But a seer can know of things which are past, and also of things which are to come, and by them shall . . . secret things be made manifest, and hidden things shall come to light" (Mosiah 8:16–17).

To Ezekiel, the prophetic contemporary of Lehi, Jehovah said: "So thou, O son of man, I have set thee a watchman unto the house of Israel; therefore thou shalt hear the word at my mouth, and warn them from me. When I say unto the wicked, O wicked man, thou shalt surely die; if thou dost not speak to warn the wicked from his way, that wicked man shall die in his iniquity; but his blood will I require at thine hand. Nevertheless, if thou warn the wicked of his way to turn from it; if he do not turn from his way, he shall die in his iniquity; but thou hast delivered thy soul" (Ezekiel 33:7–9).

Prophets are covenant spokesmen, mouthpieces for God, watchmen on the tower. They are granted the prophetic perspective to see things as they really are and as they really will be. They speak boldly in defense of virtue and powerfully in identifying and condemning evil. They fearlessly warn of social trends and doctrinal drifts among the people of the covenant. "Prophets have a way of jarring the carnal mind," declared President Spencer W. Kimball. "Too often the holy prophets are wrongly perceived as harsh and anxious to make a record in order to say, 'I told you so.' Those prophets I have known are the most loving of men. It is because of their love and integrity that they cannot modify the Lord's message merely to make people feel comfortable. They are too kind to be so cruel. I am grateful that prophets do not crave popularity."[2]

It is especially during the times of stress and distress, during the times of crisis and trauma, that the Saints of the Most High would do well to direct their attention to the words of living prophets. Their seeric vision grants them an elevated perspective, a capacity to see beyond the here and now and to plan and prepare today with "an eye of faith" toward tomorrow. Though each of us who enjoys the gift of the Holy Ghost should and must seek for the power to recognize and discern the signs of the times for what they are, the wisest among us will always and forevermore have an eye toward the First Presidency and Quorum of the Twelve Apostles and an ear attuned to their words.

In a revelation given in November 1831 to a group of men who would be called to the first Quorum of the Twelve Apostles in our dispensation, the Lord said: "*Unto you it shall be given to know the signs of the times, and the signs of the coming of the Son of Man*" (D&C 68:8–11; emphasis added).

How could the Brethren have known—except by revelation—how vital the Church welfare program was and how far-reaching its influence would be when they first established it in the 1930s? Who could have predicted the war against the home and family that would come upon us like a whirlwind when the Brethren called upon the Saints to hold a weekly family home evening in the 1960s? Could any of us have suspected what a godsend the new editions of the scriptures would prove to be in terms of arming the Saints against false educational and cultural ideas or enhancing gospel scholarship? Do we, even now, recognize the power of pure doctrine set forth in the Proclamation on the Family, a power that will do much to secure the home and preserve the family unit in even more troublesome times ahead? In a time gripped by relativism, a season that is gradually losing its hold on the doctrine of the divine Sonship, can we fully appreciate how the bold pronouncement of the prophets and seers, "The Living Christ," will yet impact a world that is desperately in need of a Savior?

We have the scriptures, the standard works, and God be praised for that. There are timeless lessons, eternal doctrines, and marvelous inspiration to be found within their covers. We can profitably study them over and over again, year in and year out, and still find new insights and new application with every reading. But the written word of God, as priceless a treasure as it is, is not what truly distinguishes the Latter-day Saints from those of other faiths. We have the living prophets, the living oracles in our midst, and their words we are to "receive as if from [the Lord's] own mouth, in all patience and faith" (D&C 21:5). The Lord of Light has given this stern warning to us: "And all they who receive the oracles of God [both the revelations and the revelators], let them beware how they hold [receive] them lest they are accounted as a light thing, and are brought under condemnation thereby, and stumble and fall when the storms descend, and the winds blow, and the rains descend, and beat upon their house" (D&C 90:5).

The Lord's living Church is indeed alive and well, for it is led by living apostles and prophets. It is to be governed by revelation—current, modern, daily revelation—and not by written documents alone. All of God's purposes for his children cannot be codified. Nothing is more fixed, set, and established than the fact that among the people of God the canon of scripture is open, flexible, and expanding, and also that the ongoing will of heaven will come through those charged to direct the destiny of this Church. The mark of distinction for The Church of Jesus Christ of Latter-day Saints is the flow of "revelation adapted to the circumstances in which the children of the kingdom are placed."[3]

Thus, the timeless counsel is to simply "follow the Brethren." Elder Boyd K. Packer told a story once of Karl G. Maeser, the man called to serve as the first president of Brigham Young University. Elder Packer explained that "on one occasion [Brother Maeser] was leading a party of young missionaries across the Alps. As they slowly ascended the steep slope, he looked back and saw a row of sticks thrust into the glacial snow to mark the one safe path across the otherwise treacherous mountains.

"Something about those sticks impressed him, and halting the company of missionaries he gestured toward them and said, 'Brethren, there stands the priesthood. They are just common sticks like the rest of us—some of them may even seem to be a little crooked, but the position they hold makes them what they are. If we step aside from the path they mark, we are lost.'"[4]

It seems to me that there are basically two avenues by which we come to enjoy the blessings of the Lord in our lives. The first is through personal righteousness and obedience to the commandments of God. The second is through loyalty to the Lord's anointed servants, for, as Jesus taught, "He that receiveth a prophet in the name of a prophet shall receive a prophet's reward" (Matthew 10:41). And that's good enough for me.

NOTES

1. See *Teachings of the Prophet Joseph Smith*, 274.

2. Conference Report, April 1978, 116.

3. *Teachings of the Prophet Joseph Smith*, 256.

4. *That All May Be Edified*, 244.

13

TREASURING UP THE WORD

A lesson I learned a number of years ago lingers in my memory. A dear friend of mine and his wife had struggled for years to have children; they had lost a couple of babies because of premature births. But to their credit and their eternal blessing, they kept trying. She became pregnant again, everything went fine for several months, and then, as had happened too often before, the baby came prematurely. We knew that the little one was struggling for life, that his lungs were not fully developed, and that all the parents had was hope and a constant prayer in their hearts. Many friends and loved ones joined with the couple in a season of fasting and prayer.

One Friday evening Shauna and I were about to leave the house to go out to dinner. We had just made our way out the front door when the phone began to ring. I suggested that Shauna wait for me in the car. On the other end of the line was my friend, the father of the struggling infant. He sounded desperate. "Bob," he said, "we need your help."

I responded quickly. "What can I do?"

He answered, "Would you please come to the hospital and give my son a blessing?"

I reacted with: "But Ted, I have all the confidence in the world in you."

"As you know," he continued, "we have given our baby a blessing, but this is so difficult for me—I feel so close to the situation and so eager for him to be made well that I just don't feel open to the Lord's will."

I need to add at this point that my friend is a righteous and good man, one who is in every way worthy of the direction of the Spirit. But I knew something about his dilemma, for in some ways I feel most inadequate in blessing my own family. Why? Because they know me best. They know my strengths, and they know my weaknesses. In addition, most of us who hold the priesthood want every good thing that can come to our family to come; it is indeed a real challenge to be spiritually objective. And so while I felt very inadequate to respond to his request, I knew where he was coming from. I agreed to hurry to the hospital.

One other detail. At the time I was serving as a counselor in a bishopric. During the preceding couple of weeks, it had been my opportunity to participate in several priesthood administrations, and in each case I had felt impressed to promise the person that he or she would be healed, and they had been. On this occasion, after hanging up the phone and before walking out to the car, I felt the need to kneel beside my bed and plead for the Lord's direction—that he would inspire me to do and say what he wanted done and said. I immediately felt an overwhelming sense of peace as the Spirit of the Lord was poured out upon me. I interpreted this to mean that I would have the privilege of being an instrument in the healing of this infant. My heart filled with deep gratitude and excitement for our friends, who would finally be able to have a child. I climbed into the car and explained Ted's request to Shauna.

The father and I were required to be adorned in hospital garb before entering the intensive care area where the baby was. We made our way to the child, Ted anointed, and I began the blessing with great confidence. I called the child by name and then said: "By the authority of the Holy Priesthood, we lay our hands upon your head, seal the anointing which you have received, and pronounce a blessing upon you. We bless you that . . ." Silence. Nothing. Nothing came to my mind. Those who know me best know that I am seldom at a loss for words, but this was different. Different from anything I had ever experienced. I seemed unable to generate a reasonable sentence, to speak even a short phrase. My mind was absolutely blank, except for the fact that I sensed and knew that my friend was anxiously waiting, as I certainly was—terribly uncomfortable with the delay, which was approaching a full minute. I pleaded with the Lord in my mind. I remember saying: "Heavenly Father, please help me. This dear man has come to me in faith, has asked for my help. Please, please forgive my sins and give me the words to speak."

My emotions were already close to the surface because of our love for this wonderful husband and wife, who only wanted to do what God had sent them to earth to do. Those feelings, coupled with the strain of the present crisis, caused the tears to come easily. And then, without warning, words came into my mind and I spoke them: "We say unto you, if you are not appointed unto death, you shall be healed." I then closed the blessing. As we left the room, Ted turned to me and said: "He's going to die, isn't he?" I nodded in the affirmative and said that I sensed that it would not be long before he would be taken home. We wept together. The infant passed away a short time later.

My heart ached in the days following the death of the baby, and we mourned for this choice couple. At the same time, there began to come into my mind and heart a sweet, peaceful sense of gratitude to God for what had taken place that evening. What the Lord had chosen to do was make me aware, through the peace of his Spirit, that his will would be done. And what he had done was to finally bring to my remembrance words, special words, words of scripture, words found in modern revelation (D&C 42:48). I felt gratitude that somewhere, sometime in the past I had taken occasion to read the scriptures, to search the revelations, and that they had, to some extent, become a part of me. And I felt to thank a gracious Lord who had fulfilled his promise that the Holy Ghost would bring to our remembrance those things that the Master had spoken to us (John 14:26).

There is great power in scripture, in the very words which the Lord and his chosen servants have spoken in the past. While we as Latter-day Saints do not worship the scripture, we revere the holy word and know that it can and does have a lasting and lifting impact on our lives. In speaking of the power of the Book of Mormon, President Ezra Taft Benson taught, "It is important that in our teaching [and, I would add, in our personal lives] we make use of the language of holy writ. . . . The words and the way they are used in the Book of Mormon by the Lord should become our source of understanding and should be used by us in teaching gospel principles."[1]

In a revelation given to Oliver Cowdery and David Whitmer, the Savior explained the nature of the prophetic word: "These words [the revelations in the Doctrine and Covenants, and, by extension, the words of all scripture] are not of men nor of man, but of me; wherefore, you shall testify they are of me and not of man; for it is my voice which speaketh them unto you; for they are given by my Spirit unto you, and by my power you can read them one to another; and save it were by my power you could not have them; wherefore, you can testify that you have heard my voice, and know my words" (D&C 18:34–36). In applying this grand principle, and after a lifetime of immersion in holy writ, Elder Bruce R. McConkie testified in his last address to the Church: "In speaking of these wondrous things [the Atonement] I shall use my own words, though you may think they are the words of scripture, words spoken by other Apostles and prophets.

"True it is they were first proclaimed by others, but they are now mine, for the Holy Spirit of God has borne witness to me that they are true, and it is now as though the Lord had revealed them to me in the first instance. I have thereby heard his voice and know his word."[2]

It is when the scriptures have become ours, when they have been read and studied and memorized and quoted and paraphrased and cited again and again in our own ministries, that they begin to have a transforming effect upon our souls. It is when they are written upon our hearts that the *doctrines* contained therein begin to unfold divine *principles* in our lives. We cannot lead the Church or direct our homes on the basis of rules and regulations alone, nor do we dare attempt to codify every case and live our lives on the basis of legal precedent. Rather, we seek to know the gospel well enough to be able to live and lead by principle. No handbook, no collection of regulations can be written to handle every imaginable situation that will arise. Rather, we seek the Spirit for direction (D&C 46:2) and strive to ask ourselves, "What is the principle involved here?" and act accordingly.[3]

It is a knowledge of the doctrine and the principles that preserves us, that keeps us from deception in a day when our ears are bombarded by a babble of voices. In his Olivet discourse, the Master counseled that "whoso treasureth up my word, shall not be deceived" (Joseph Smith–Matthew 1:37). In our day that same Lord has spoken: "Behold, I am Jesus Christ, the Savior of the world. Treasure these things up in your hearts, and let the solemnities of eternity rest upon your minds" (D&C 43:34; compare 6:20). And note this remarkable promise concerning knowing the will of God: "Neither take ye thought beforehand what ye shall say; but *treasure up in your minds continually the words of life,* and it shall be given you in the very hour that portion that shall be meted unto every man" (D&C 84:85; emphasis added).

In warning priesthood leaders to be discerning in regard to sensational writings afloat among the Latter-day Saints, President Harold B. Lee said: "There are among us many loose writings predicting the calamities which are about to overtake us. Some of these have been publicized as though they were necessary to wake up the world to the horrors about to overtake us. Many of these are from sources upon which there cannot be unquestioned reliance.

"Are you priesthood bearers aware of the fact that we need no such publications to be forewarned, if we were only conversant with what the scriptures have already spoken to us in plainness?

"Let me give you the sure word of prophecy on which you should rely for your guide instead of these strange sources which may have great political implications." President Lee then encouraged the Saints to study the word of the Lord as contained in Joseph Smith–Matthew and in sections 38, 45, 101, and 133 of the Doctrine and Covenants. He added: "Brethren, these are some of the writings with which you should concern yourselves, rather than commentaries that may come from those whose information may not be the most reliable and whose motives may be subject to question. And may I say, parenthetically, most of such writers are not handicapped by having any authentic information on their writings."[4]

It's worth emphasizing that "the sure word of prophecy" upon which we are to rely is to be found in modern revelation. I have been fascinated with the fact that, more often than not, those who become obsessed with the signs of the times and who seek to specialize in clarifying the details of the same tend to spend a great deal of time in such books as Isaiah, Ezekiel, Daniel, or Revelation. Now, to be sure, these books are a part of our standard works and these prophets (and their words) are to be revered by the people of the covenant. At the same time, however, those of us living in this final dispensation would do well to focus our greater efforts in scripture study upon those things which the Lord has communicated to us through modern prophets (D&C 84:54–61).

"In each dispensation," President Marion G. Romney taught, "the Lord has revealed anew the principles of the gospel. So that while the records of past dispensations, insofar as they are uncorrupted, testify to the truths of the gospel, still each dispensation has had revealed in its day sufficient truth to guide the people of the new dispensation, independent of the records of the past.

"I do not wish to discredit in any manner the records we

have of the truths revealed by the Lord in past dispensations. What I now desire is to impress upon our minds that the gospel, as revealed to the Prophet Joseph Smith, is complete and is the word direct from heaven to this dispensation. It alone is sufficient to teach us the principles of eternal life. It is the truth revealed, the commandments given in this dispensation through modern prophets by which we are to be governed."[5]

During the time when I worked as a counselor for LDS Social Services many years ago, I found myself going from interview to interview without much of a break. Not only did I finish the day absolutely exhausted, but I also feared that I was not giving the very best I had to each client. And so I changed my schedule a bit. I asked the secretaries to arrange my appointments in such a way that there were fifteen to thirty minutes between sessions. After an interview would conclude, I would make a few notes on the discussion; then I would take out the Book of Mormon and read. By the time the next interview began, I found myself rested and invigorated. Likewise, during the difficult years when some of our loved ones were struggling to find their way, I rediscovered the scriptures as a divine source of comfort, solace, and direction. More times than I can remember, I searched the pages of holy writ with a zeal known only to those who know such pain. As I did so, not only did I find "new writing" (1 Nephi 16:29) with each reading, but also new hope, new resolve, new perspective in dealing with the present crisis.

And so it has been in regard to teaching my classes, leading my ward or stake, or counseling my children. I have come to know the unspeakable value of treasuring up the words of life, of reading and then pondering upon the implications of ancient and modern scripture. I have observed that there is a wisdom that comes to those who treasure up the words of life, a judgment and a sense of propriety that characterize those who have prepared themselves by study for their own individual ministry, a spiritual power that accompanies the teaching of those who rely on the words of eternal life. And there is a serenity of soul that flows from such a person, a serenity that enables the individual and those he loves to move forward with confidence during times of trouble.

NOTES

1. *A Witness and a Warning*, 31–32.

2. Conference Report, April 1985, 9.

3. Boyd K. Packer, *The Things of the Soul*, 64–65.

4. Conference Report, October 1972, 128.

5. "A Glorious Promise," 2.

14

FAITH IN A DAY OF UNBELIEF

I have been thinking about faith a great deal lately. My thoughts have returned to an address delivered by President Harold B. Lee at a student fireside in Logan, Utah, in 1971. "Fifty years ago or more," he said, "when I was a missionary, our greatest responsibility was to defend the great truth that the Prophet Joseph Smith was divinely called and inspired and that the Book of Mormon was indeed the word of God. But even at that time there were the unmistakable evidences that there was coming into the religious world actually a question about the Bible and about the divine calling of the Master himself. Now, [many] years later, our greatest responsibility and anxiety is to defend the divine mission of our Lord and Master, Jesus Christ, for all about us, even among those who claim to be professors of the Christian faith, are those not willing to stand squarely in defense of the great truth that our Lord and Master, Jesus Christ, was indeed the Son of God."[1]

Clearly, there are few things as desperately needed in our day than faith—faith in the unseen, or as one astute observer of Christianity has noted, "Faith that bridges the chasm between what our minds can know and what our souls aspire after."[2]

Faith is not whimpering acquiescence, not timid and spineless hope for happiness, for pie-in-the-sky in the great-by-and-by. Faith is active. Faith is powerful. Faith is based on evidence, internal evidence, the kind of evidence that men and women acquire who search and pray and open themselves to the Infinite, who refuse to yield to cynicism or arrogance.

There is a sense in which faith requires us to act in the face of (what the world would consider to be) the absurd. Abraham was asked to put to death his beloved and long-awaited son, Isaac, the one hope Abraham had of fulfilling the promise that his posterity would be as numberless as the sands upon the seashore or the stars in the heavens. Jehovah had spoken. Abraham had entered the realm of divine experience, knew the voice of the Lord, and knew what he had encountered was real. Therefore, when the awful assignment came to offer up Isaac in sacrifice, he obeyed, even though, rationally speaking, there was no way the promises could thereafter be realized. But the Father of the Faithful had implicit trust in his God, "accounting that God was able to raise [Isaac] up, even from the dead" (Hebrews 11:19). Abraham knew God, and he knew his purposes; the finite mind yielded to the Infinite, knowing fully that "whatever God requires is right, no matter what it is, although we may not see the reason thereof till long after the events transpire."[3]

His leap of faith was prerequisite to his ascent to glory.

I am shocked and often surprised by the ways some of us often use the word *faith*. I hear a missionary in Vienna say: "Come on, Elder (or Sister), where's your faith? Why, if we had the faith we could baptize this whole city!" I watch with some sorrow as well-meaning but insensitive souls explain to a grieving mother and father that if the family had sufficient faith, their fifteen-year-old daughter, who has struggled with multiple sclerosis for five years, would not be forced to suffer longer. Faith is not the power of positive thinking. Faith is not the personal resolve that enables us to will some difficult situation into existence. Faith is not always the capacity to turn tragedy into celebration. Faith is a principle of power, of God's power. We do not generate faith on our own, for "it is the gift of God" (Ephesians 2:8). We do not act ourselves into faith, for faith comes to us by the Spirit (Moroni 10:1), given by God to suit his purposes and bless his children.

People act in faith when they act according to the will of God. To say that another way, I can have sufficient faith to move Mount Timpanogos to the middle of Utah Lake only when I know that the Lord wants it moved! I can have faith or power to touch the hearts of men and women with my testimony of the truth only when they are prepared and readied for the word. Even the Master could not perform miracles in the midst of a people steeped in spiritual indifference. "A prophet is not without honour," Jesus said in speaking of his own reception in Nazareth, "save in his own country, and in his own house. *And he did not many mighty works there because of their unbelief*" (Matthew 13:57–58; emphasis added). Similarly, the prophet-leader Mormon loved his people and poured out his soul in prayer in their behalf; "nevertheless, it was without faith, because of the hardness of their hearts" (Mormon 3:12). Someone watching from the sidelines, unaware of what faith really is, might have cried out: "Come on, Mormon, where's your faith?"

Again, acting by faith is acting according to the will of the Lord. I remember very well one warm June evening in Louisiana, only a few months after I had returned from a mission, sitting with my mom and dad watching television. The phone rang, and my father was quickly summoned to the hospital to give a priesthood blessing to someone. A sixteen-year-old boy, a friend of my younger sister, had suddenly collapsed on the softball field and had been rushed to the hospital. My dad was told that the boy had been diagnosed with a strange, degenerative nerve disease and that if something didn't happen soon he would die. We rushed to the hospital, took the elevator to the fifth floor, and hurried through the doors that opened to the waiting room. We were greeted by the sorrowing of friends and loved ones; the young man had died. We did our best to console the mourners and then made our way home.

As we walked in the back door, my sister asked, "How is he?" I answered that her friend had passed away. She came right back with: "Well, why didn't you raise him from the dead?" Being the seasoned and experienced returned missionary that I was, having most of the answers to life's hard questions, I stuttered for a second and then turned to my father: "Yeah, why didn't we raise him from the dead?"

Dad's answer was kind but firm. It was also very instructive: "Because the Spirit of the Lord didn't prompt us to do so," he said. I have to admit that at that moment a piece of cynicism made its way into my conscious thoughts, and I said to myself: "That's a bit of a cop-out, isn't it?" In the years that followed, however, I came to know something about my dad's faith: he had been with his father when in fact the Spirit had prompted, and the dead had been raised to life again. He knew when to move and when not to move. He had faith.

In late 1838 Wilford Woodruff was traveling to Zion to assume his new assignment in the Quorum of the Twelve. On the journey his wife, Phoebe, was overcome with a high fever and lay upon the point of death. While Sister Woodruff was prepared to face death with courage, her husband was not eager to let her go. At a certain point, however, Sister Woodruff seems to have breathed her last and passed away, and the sisters who had gathered at the home began to weep. "The spirit and power of God began to rest upon me," Elder Woodruff said, "until, for the first time during her sickness, faith filled my soul, although she lay before me as one dead." He anointed his wife with oil and in the name of Jesus Christ rebuked the power of death and commanded her to live. "Her spirit returned to her body, and from that hour she was made whole; and we all felt to praise the name of God, and to trust in Him and to keep His commandments." Sister Woodruff later explained that after her spirit left her body she was given the choice to either move on in her eternal journey or to return to mortality. She chose to return. "At the moment that decision was made," her husband said, "the power of faith rested upon me, and when I administered unto her, her spirit entered her tabernacle."[4]

Joseph Smith taught that working by faith is working by the power of mental exertion rather than physical force.[5] I am persuaded that the mental exertion of which he spoke is not merely a cognitive exercise, but rather a demanding, strenuous effort, a spiritual search to know the will of God and then to accept and abide by that will. "Working by faith is not the mere speaking of a few well-chosen words," Elder Bruce R. McConkie has written. "Anyone with the power of speech could have commanded the rotting corpse of Lazarus to come forth, but only one whose power was greater than death could bring life again to the brother of Mary and Martha. Nor is working by faith merely a mental desire, however strong, that some eventuality should occur. . . . Faith cannot be exercised contrary to the order of heaven or contrary to the will and purposes of him whose power it is. *Men work by faith when they are in tune with the Spirit and when what they seek to do by mental exertion and by the spoken word is the mind and will of the Lord.*"[6]

The Lord asks us to move forward on the path of life on the basis of what has been made known through prophets. We cannot always see the end from the beginning. We cannot always act in the face of the observable or the demonstrable. In many cases, believing must precede seeing. Indeed, the revelations affirm that as we search diligently, pray always, and *be believing*, all things will work together for our good (D&C 90:24). We are further counseled to doubt not because we see not, for we receive no witness until after the trial of our faith (Ether 12:6). This is the nature of the leap of faith, a leap from the safe and the secure to the anticipated and the hoped for (Alma 32:21). The disciples of Christ are not called upon to proceed wholly in the dark, to leap from the precipice without evidence of deliverance. Rather, we are asked to rely upon the unseen, to trust in the quiet but persistent whisperings of the Spirit, to lean upon the prophetic promises. In the words of Elder Harold B. Lee, we must "learn to walk to the edge of the light, and perhaps a few steps into the darkness, and [we] will find that the light will appear and move ahead of [us]."[7]

Faith has its own type of discipline. Some things that are obvious to the faithful sound like the gibberish of alien tongues to the faithless. The discipline of faith, the concentrated and consecrated effort to become single to God, has its own reward, a reward that includes the expansion of the mind.

Such persons come to be filled with light and are able in time to comprehend "all things" (D&C 88:67).

It is worth considering the words of a revelation given in Kirtland, Ohio. Having encouraged the Saints to call a solemn assembly, the Lord continued: "And as all have not faith, seek ye diligently and teach one another words of wisdom; . . . seek learning, even by study and also by faith" (D&C 88:118). We note that the counsel to seek learning out of the best books is prefaced by the negative clause, "And as all *have not* faith . . ." One wonders whether the Master did not intend something such as the following: Since all do not have sufficient faith— that is, since they have not "matured in their religious convictions" enough to learn by any other means[8]—then they must seek learning by study, the use of the rational processes alone. In other words, if all *did* have the requisite faith, then what?

Perhaps learning by studying from the best books would then be greatly enhanced by revelation. Honest truth seekers would learn things in this way that they could not know otherwise. Could this be what Joseph Smith meant when he taught that "the best way to obtain truth and wisdom is not to ask it from books, but to go to God in prayer, and obtain teaching"?[9]

It is surely in this same context that another of the Prophet's famous yet little-understood statements finds meaning: "Could you gaze into heaven five minutes," he declared, "you would know more than you would by reading all that ever was written on the subject" of life after death.[10]

"I believe in study," President Marion G. Romney stated. "I believe that men learn much through study. As a matter of fact, it has been my observation that they learn little concerning things as they are, as they were, or as they are to come without study. *I also believe, however, and know, that learning by study is greatly accelerated by faith.*"[11]

And so as we move into the twenty-first century and as we are called upon to face difficult challenges—we move forward in faith. Faith in Jesus Christ is trust in Jesus Christ. It is reliance. It is confidence. We have faith in him in that we believe he is who the prophets say he is. We have faith in him in that we believe he has done for humankind what no other mortal could ever do—he "hath abolished death, and hath brought life and immortality to light through the gospel" (2 Timothy 1:10). We have faith in him in that we feel to trust in his promises and his purposes. We have faith in him, even as Joseph the Seer had faith. At a very difficult time, the Prophet wrote to Emma: "God is my friend. In him I shall find comfort. I have given my life into his hands. I am prepared to go at his call. I desire to be with Christ. I count not my life dear to me, only to do his will."[12] And we have faith that Christ will come again to earth, will remove wickedness, right all of the terrible wrongs of this existence, and wipe away all tears.

> *Jesus, lover of my soul,*
> *Let me to thy bosom fly,*
> *While the nearer waters roll,*
> *While the tempest still is high.*
> *Hide me, O my Savior, hide,*
> *Till the storm of life is past.*
> *Safe into the haven guide;*
> *Oh, receive my soul at last.*
>
> *Other refuge have I none;*
> *Hangs my helpless soul on thee.*
> *Leave, oh, leave me not alone;*

Still support and comfort me.
All my trust on thee is stayed;
All my help from thee I bring.
Cover my defenseless head
With the shadow of thy wing.[13]

NOTES

1. LDS Student Association fireside, 10 October 1971.

2. Malcolm Muggeridge, *Jesus: The Man Who Lives*, 20.

3. *Teachings of the Prophet Joseph Smith*, 256.

4. *Leaves from My Journal*, 54–55.

5. *Lectures on Faith*, 7:3.

6. *A New Witness for the Articles of Faith*, 191–92; emphasis added.

7. Cited in Boyd K. Packer, *The Holy Temple*, 184.

8. Harold B. Lee, Conference Report, April 1968, 129.

9. *Teachings of the Prophet Joseph Smith*, 191.

10. *Teachings of the Prophet Joseph Smith*, 324.

11. *Learning for the Eternities*, 72; emphasis added.

12. *The Personal Writings of Joseph Smith*, 239; punctuation and capitalization standardized.

13. Charles Wesley, "Jesus, Lover of My Soul," in *Hymns of The Church of Jesus Christ of Latter-day Saints*, no. 102.

15

OIL IN OUR LAMPS

Elder Harold B. Lee related a story that teaches a timeless lesson. "The story opens," he said, "with a young woman on the train, alone with her thoughts, on her way to visit her dying father. For the hundredth time she opened her purse, took out the telegram that read simply, 'Father critically ill. Come at once. Mother,' and all through the journey the daughter prayed that the Lord would keep him alive until she could arrive and see him again; then somewhat guiltily she had to say to herself, 'Well, over the years we have taken father more or less [as] just a matter of course.' He was a necessity; he provided our food and our clothes and our shelter, but somehow now to realize that he was in imminent danger of slipping away, being taken by death, caused a longing that she could be close to him again, that she could roll back the years and see him again as she had seen him in her childhood days. Father was in a coma, still alive when she arrived, but a few hours later he slipped quietly away. She was assigned by the family to the task of going through his personal papers and taking care of what the family called the 'unfinished business.'

"She went carefully to her task to make sure that there was nothing that he wished to have done that would be left undone. As she searched in an inside pocket of his coat, she came upon a crumpled bit of paper which showed the effects of having been removed and read, and folded and unfolded many times. This crumpled piece of paper was a message from a young girl whom her father had befriended, and this letter was a letter of appreciation to this great, noble father. Although this other little girl was not his daughter, he had seemingly clung to the message which this letter conveyed as something of a satisfaction that he hadn't received from his own. The little girl had poured out her heart in gratitude that he had come at a crisis in her life, and she openly expressed her love for his thoughtfulness and kindness to her and his considera- tion. The daughter laid down the paper and wept because she realized that his own daughter had failed to give her father what this other girl had given and the thing for which he had longed so much. 'Unfinished business' but unfortunately the kind of business that she was not permitted to finish. How she wished that she could have rolled back the clock and had a chance to live over some of the years, to have made the life of her father more happy and more joyous than she had done."[1]

Because the past no longer belongs to us, we can do little about it except to repent and learn from our mistakes. Because the future is also out of our reach, we can do little about it except to "improve our time" (Alma 34:33) in this life and make necessary preparations for tomorrow. Today is precious. As we sing in the hymn,

> *Time flies on wings of lightning;*
> *We cannot call it back.*
> *It comes, then passes forward*
> *Along its onward track.*
> *And if we are not mindful,*
> *The chance will fade away,*

> *For life is quick in passing.*
> *'Tis as a single day.*[2]

In ancient Israel a wedding ceremony could be quite an event. The groom would arrive at the bride's house, and the processional would then continue to the groom's house. When the wedding took place at night, lamps or torches were employed. The torches were generally on a long pole and had oil-drenched rags at the end. Clay lamps may also have been used, but they would not have been as useful as the torches. Interestingly, the main characters in the parable of the ten virgins in Matthew 25 are designated as ten virgins (or bridesmaids, ladies in waiting), meaning presumably ten people who have kept themselves from the taints of the world. They are divided into two groups—not righteous and wicked, but rather wise (or provident) and unwise (or foolish).

All of the virgins started out right, for the account indicates that they "took their lamps and went forth to meet the bridegroom." But the unwise are found unprepared in regard to what it takes to keep the light of God burning in their lives. They are careless; they do not exercise enough foresight to prepare for what lies ahead. The level of oil (often symbolic of the Holy Spirit) within their lamps could thus represent the degree to which they had cultivated the influence of the Holy Spirit to navigate life's shoals and to empower them in meeting life's challenges. When the crucial moment has arrived, the time of preparation is over.

When the cry was sounded concerning the coming of the bridegroom, everyone scurried about. And, sadly, the unwise virgins were not able to sustain light in their lives because they had not prepared properly. One is tempted to read this parable and ask: "Why don't the wise virgins simply share with the foolish ones? Why not extend yourself a little bit?" Surely, we reason, if people could learn to share what they have then everyone would be prepared for the coming of the bridegroom, that is, a time of judgment. Sadly, Jesus points out that there are some things that one cannot loan to a neighbor on the spur of the moment. Can we loan what we learn and what we develop over the years as we lift and strengthen and love others? Can we share the product of developing meaningful relationships?

I gained a whole new appreciation for this parable a number of years ago. While I was serving as a priesthood leader, a husband and wife came in to see me. They were both distressed about the state of their marriage and family; things seemed to be coming apart in their lives. "How can I help?" I asked.

"We need more spirituality in our home," the wife answered.

I asked a few questions. "How often do you pray as a family?"

They answered that their hectic schedules precluded any kind of family prayer.

"Have you been able to hold family home evening?"

"Bill and I bowl on Monday nights" was the response.

"Do you read the scriptures as a family or as individuals?"

The answer from the husband: "Reading hurts my eyes."

"Well, then, how can I help you?"

Again the reply: "We want the Spirit in our lives."

It was as though they were saying to me, "Brother Millet, could you reach down into your heart and lend us five years of daily prayer, ten years of regular scripture study, and fifteen years of family spiritual activities?" I couldn't do it. I realized dramatically that there are some things that we simply cannot share. President Spencer W. Kimball pointed out that "the foolish [virgins] asked the others to share their oil, but spiritual preparedness cannot be shared in an instant. . . . This was not selfishness or unkindness. The kind of oil that is needed to illuminate the way and light up the darkness is not shareable. . . . In our lives the oil of preparedness is accumulated drop by drop in righteous living."[3]

Individuals who choose to ignore parental teachings or societal standards; persons young and old who refuse to bridle their passions and thereby act immaturely and irresponsibly; fathers and mothers who make little effort to teach their children right from wrong; people of all walks of life who turn a deaf ear to the inner sense of morality and decency within them and who in general show little reverence for life—these all find their lamps devoid of oil in the time of crisis.

Just as many of the small lamps in the Middle East require a careful and methodical effort to fill them, so in our own lives we need to build our reservoirs of faith and spiritual depth gradually, drop by tiny drop. Every noble deed, every prayer, every period of sincere fasting, every lesson we teach and testimony we bear, every moment of quiet reflection on things of eternity add to the reservoir. Some people try to defy the law of the harvest (Galatians 6:7–8), to reap where they have not sown, to enjoy the fruits of labors that were never performed or were performed shabbily. Or, as in this parable, some of us seek desperately, at the time of crisis, to compensate for long-term neglect through sudden bursts of effort. Jesus is teaching that the way to peace and preparation is not through spiritual marathons at the last hour, but rather through consistent and steady personal progress throughout our lives.

The time of the coming of the Bridegroom, like the day of our own death, is not known precisely. Death is something all of us would avoid, if we could, but we cannot. It is inevitable. When we face it, if we are unprepared to meet God, it will be a day of remorse and personal agony, for "the torment of disappointment in the mind of man is as exquisite as a lake burning with fire and brimstone."[4]

"The great misery of departed spirits in the world of spirits, where they go after death, is to know that they come short of the glory that others enjoy and that they might have enjoyed themselves, and they are their own accusers."[5]

Many years ago I was called to serve as bishop of our home ward. It was a terribly busy time for me and my young family. I was serving as the director of the institute of religion and had supervisory responsibility for seminary in five different stakes. Added to this was the fact that I had started a doctoral degree in a discipline where I had little or no background; I don't think I had ever taken an undergraduate course in the field, and so a good deal of remedial work was necessary. Days were long, and nights were extremely short. I remember, for example, counseling as a bishop with a struggling married couple until about two o'clock in the morning, then sitting down at my desk in the bishop's office, pulling my notes together, and beginning a major paper that was due in six hours. This happened more than once.

It seemed as if we would never see the light at the end of the tunnel. I can't count the number of times during those challenging years that I said to my wife, Shauna, "This is crazy! Why am I doing this? I don't need this. I'm going to drop out of this doctoral program." She would quietly, lovingly, but firmly respond, "No, sweetheart, you're not going to quit.

We've come too far to quit, and, besides, you'll need this degree in years to come."

A young family moved into our ward, and the executive secretary scheduled an appointment for the bishopric to meet with them. After we had chatted cordially for a few minutes and discovered where they were from, where they had lived before, and so forth, we asked about their employment. "Oh," the husband said, "I'm here working on a Ph.D." Then he added this rather interesting comment: "Bishop, I don't know if you know anything about this degree program I've been admitted to, but it's very intense, one that will require all of my time and energies to complete." The program, by the way, was the same one I was working in. I asked him to tell me more about it.

He provided much detail and then said, "And so, Bishop, it seems to me that it would be wise for me to be allowed to work at my education full-time without the distraction or drain of a Church calling. Maybe by the time I'm finishing up we can find something that would fit my talent and background, something that would require a minimal amount of effort." The three members of the bishopric each suggested that perhaps he could find the time for some small assignment even before then, but he indicated that he didn't feel comfortable even taking a home teaching responsibility. We complied with his wishes. I watched with much interest and sorrow over the next few years: despite the efforts of many to involve the man in ward functions, he maintained but a distant connection to the Church. I don't know how he and his wife are doing now, many years later, but I worry that things still may not be quite right for them spiritually.

When the Lord Jesus comes in his glory, then "shall the

parable be fulfilled which I spake concerning the ten virgins. For they that are wise and have received the truth, and have taken the Holy Spirit for their guide, and have not been deceived—verily I say unto you, they shall not be hewn down and cast into the fire, but shall abide the day" (D&C 45:56–57). "Wherefore, be faithful, praying always, having your lamps trimmed and burning, and oil with you, that you may be ready at the coming of the Bridegroom" (D&C 33:17).

The gradual acquisition of oil in our lamps of faith prepares us to read the signs of the times, a task that is difficult and requires significant judgment and discernment. Those who have searched the scriptures and pondered the words of the prophets from days gone by, those who give diligent heed to the words of eternal life as those words come forth from current apostles and prophets, and those whose faith in the Savior entails a genuine loyalty to seers and revelators who now lead and will yet lead the restored Church—these are they who will be enabled to read the signs of the times and be prepared for that which is to be.

In one sense, to read the signs of the times is to perceive the unfolding of God's divine drama in these last days. It is to understand that this is the day long awaited by the prophets of old and by the messengers of heaven, when God would pour out knowledge and power from on high "by the unspeakable gift of the Holy Ghost," knowledge "that has not been revealed since the world was until now" (D&C 121:26). On the other hand, to read the signs of the times in our day is to read the signs of wear and tear in the faces of those who have chosen to love and give devoted service to either questionable or diabolical causes. Error and wickedness take their terrible tolls upon the hearts and countenances of those who choose divergent paths; the wheels of waywardness grind away slowly but inexorably to desensitize the character and thereby rob a person of peace of mind. To read the signs of the times is, in part, to recognize that Alma spoke a profound truth when he counseled a wayward son that "wickedness never was happiness" (Alma 41:10).

To read the signs of the times in our day is to make a decision in favor of the society of Zion and the Church of the Lamb of God (1 Nephi 14:10)—this in contrast to a decision to enter or perpetuate Babylon. Each city, Zion and Babylon, makes definite demands of its citizens, and as the time approaches the millennial day each of these communities will insist upon the total devotion and consecration of its citizenry. To read the signs of the times is to recognize that in the future fewer and fewer Latter-day Saints will be "lukewarm" (Revelation 3:16); that the myopic and misguided of the religious world will grow in cynicism and confusion; that the ungodly will, as time goes by, sink ever deeper into a despair known only to those who revel in iniquity; that wickedness will widen and malevolence multiply until the citizens of Babylon seal themselves to him who is the father of all lies.

To read the signs of the times is also to know that "Zion must arise and put on her beautiful garments" (D&C 82:14); that the Church of the Lamb will continue to require the tithes, offerings, and donations of its members until that day when theirs is a full and consecrated life; and that through yielding their hearts unto God and thereby giving all to the Lord through his Church, the Saints of the Most High will establish a heaven on earth and receive the glorious assurance of exaltation in the highest heaven.

NOTES

1. "Cram for Life's Final Examination," 1–2.
2. Robert B. Baird, "Improve the Shining Moments," in *Hymns of The Church of Jesus Christ of Latter-day Saints*, no. 226.
3. *Faith Precedes the Miracle*, 255–56.
4. *Teachings of the Prophet Joseph Smith*, 357.
5. *Teachings of the Prophet Joseph Smith*, 310–11.

16

WHEN WILL THE END COME?

I remember very well a particular night in my past. I was in the fourth grade, was sitting in the living room one warm evening with my parents, and was pretending to be engrossed in the television program Mom and Dad were viewing. My mind, however, was not on that program. Instead, my thoughts were on something else—the second coming of Christ. I know that sounds a little strange for a fourth grader, but then, I've always been a little strange. As I recall, I had heard a powerful sermon in Church about the Second Coming, and it had really gotten my attention. In fact, it scared me to death! Added to that was the fact that I had dreamed about that future event just a few nights before and been horrified in my dream because of visions of flies and maggots and death and bodies coming out of graves and the burning of the earth. For someone like me with so very little understanding, it seemed like a pretty bizarre and frightening thing.

For some reason, I was obsessed with the idea that because no one really knew the exact time of the Lord's coming in glory, it was going to happen at any time, any minute now. I wasn't ready. I wanted to live longer, to grow up, to go on a mission, to get married and have a family, to get something done before everything came crashing down. As I think back on those moments in the living room, I can still recall how tense I was, how fast my heart was beating. And then, without warning, a car horn sounded across the street. But it wasn't a car horn to me; it was a trumpet, an angel's trumpet. It was here. I jumped up from the sofa and cried out: "It's time. He's here!"

My startled dad responded: "Who's here?"

"Jesus," I said.

He and Mom managed to calm me down and explain a few things, including the fact that I would probably be able to go to the movies the next Saturday. All was well. It would be a while before we would welcome our Savior to earth.

In some ways my experience as a fourth grader is not too unlike what many grownups feel today. For them, the coming of Jesus Christ to earth is something they fear, something they don't really know much about, something they would just as soon put off indefinitely. In a modern revelation, the Master explained that "if ye are prepared ye shall not fear" (D&C 38:30). As we have discussed before, such preparation has much to do with cultivating the Spirit, keeping our covenants, creating a loving environment in the home, and bringing up our children and grandchildren in light and truth. In addition, we prepare ourselves for what lies ahead by studying the holy word and listening attentively to those charged to guide the destiny of the Lord's kingdom. In short, the more we know, the better off we are, and the less anxiety and worry we experience. In that spirit, let's review a few of the fundamental matters associated with the second coming of the Lord.

Jesus came to earth as a mortal being in the meridian of time. He taught the gospel, bestowed divine authority,

organized the Church, and suffered and died as an infinite
atoning sacrifice for the sins of the world. He stated that he
would come again, would return not as the meek and lowly
Nazarene but as the Lord of Sabaoth, the Lord of Hosts, the
Lord of Armies. His second coming is thus spoken of as his
coming "in glory," meaning, in his true identity as the God of
all creation, the Redeemer and Judge. His second coming is
described as both *great* and *dreadful*—great for those who have
been true and faithful and therefore look forward to his coming, and dreadful to those who have done despite to the spirit
of grace and who therefore hope against hope that he will
never return. The Second Coming in glory is in fact "the end
of the world," meaning the end of worldliness, the destruction
of the wicked (Joseph Smith–Matthew 1:4, 31).[1]

At this coming the wicked will be destroyed, the righteous
quickened and caught up to meet him, and the earth trans-
formed from a fallen telestial orb to a terrestrial, paradisiacal
sphere. We will live and move about among new heavens and
a new earth. The Second Coming will initiate the millennial
reign.

The scriptures speak of the Master returning as "a thief in
the night" (1 Thessalonians 5:2; 2 Peter 3:10). It is true that
no mortal man has known, does now know, or will yet know
the precise day of the Lord's second advent. This is true for
prophets and apostles as well as the rank and file of society and
the Church. The Lord did not reveal even to Joseph Smith the
precise day and time of his coming (D&C 130:14–17). Elder
M. Russell Ballard has observed: "I am called as one of the
apostles to be a special witness of Christ in these exciting, trying times, and I do not know when He is going to come again.
As far as I know, none of my brethren in the Council of the

Twelve or even in the First Presidency knows. And I would humbly suggest to you . . . that if we do not know, then nobody knows, no matter how compelling their arguments or how reasonable their calculations. . . .

"I believe when the Lord says 'no man' knows, it really means that no man knows. You should be extremely wary of anyone who claims to be an exception to divine decree."[2]

On the other hand, the Saints are promised that if they are in tune with the Spirit, they can know the season. The apostle Paul chose the descriptive analogy of a pregnant woman about to deliver. She may not know the exact hour or day when the birth is to take place, but one thing she knows for sure: it will be soon. It *must* be soon! The impressions and feelings and signs within her own body so testify.

In that day, surely the Saints of the Most High, the members of the body of Christ, will be pleading for the Lord to deliver the travailing earth, to bring an end to corruption and degradation, to introduce an era of peace and righteousness. And those who give heed to the words of scripture, and especially to the living oracles, will stand as "the children of light, and the children of the day," those who "are not of the night, nor of darkness" (1 Thessalonians 5:5). In a modern revelation the Savior declared: "And again, verily I say unto you, the coming of the Lord draweth nigh, and *it overtaketh the world as a thief in the night*—therefore, gird up your loins, that you may be the children of light, and that day shall not overtake you as a thief" (D&C 106:4–5; emphasis added).

As we noted in an earlier chapter, the Lord spoke to those brethren who would eventually be called to the first Quorum of the Twelve Apostles in this dispensation: "And unto you it shall be given to know the signs of the times, and the signs of the coming of the Son of Man" (D&C 68:11). As we move closer to the end of time, we would do well to live in such a manner that we can discern the signs of the times; we would be wise also to keep our eyes fixed and our ears riveted on those called to direct the destiny of this Church. The Prophet Joseph Smith pointed out that a particular man who claimed prophetic powers "has not seen the sign of the Son of Man as foretold by Jesus. Neither has any man, nor will any man, till after the sun shall have been darkened and the moon bathed in blood. For the Lord hath not shown me any such sign, and as the prophet saith, so it must be: 'Surely the Lord God will do nothing, but he revealeth his secret unto his servants the prophets.'"[3]

In November 1831 the early elders of the Church were given their authorization to preach the gospel: "Go ye into all the world, preach the gospel to every creature, acting in the authority which I have given you, baptizing in the name of the Father, and of the Son, and of the Holy Ghost" (D&C 68:8). Also: "For, verily, the sound must go forth from this place into all the world, and unto the uttermost parts of the earth—the gospel must be preached unto every creature, with signs following them that believe" (D&C 58:64). It is true that every person must have the opportunity to hear the gospel, either here or hereafter. In fact, John the Revelator saw that before the Second Coming there would be kings and priests in every nation, kindred, tongue, and people (Revelation 5:9–10). This means that a nucleus of faithful Latter-day Saints will have been established in every land so that the blessings of the House of the Lord are available to them.[4] But not all people will have the privilege of hearing the gospel as mortals, and not all will have that privilege before the Second

Coming. The great day of gathering—the day when millions upon millions will come into the true fold of God—is millennial (1 Nephi 22:25–26; 3 Nephi 21:23–28).[5]

There may be some wisdom in speaking of the Second *Comings* of the Lord Jesus Christ, three of which are preliminary appearances or comings to select groups, and one of which is to the whole world. The Lord will make a preliminary appearance *to his temple in Independence, Jackson County, Missouri.* This seems to be a private appearance to those holding the keys of power in the earthly kingdom. President Charles W. Penrose observed that the Savior "will come to the Temple prepared for him, and his faithful people will behold his face, hear his voice, and gaze upon his glory. From his own lips they will receive further instructions for the development and beautifying of Zion and for the extension and sure stability of his kingdom."[6]

The Lord will make an appearance *at Adam-ondi-Ahman,* "the place where Adam shall come to visit his people, or the Ancient of Days shall sit" (D&C 116). For one thing, this grand council will be a large sacrament meeting, a time when the Son of Man will partake of the fruit of the vine once more with his earthly friends. And who will be in attendance? The revelations specify Moroni, Elias, John the Baptist, Elijah, Abraham, Isaac, Jacob, Joseph, Adam, Peter, James, John, "and also," the Savior clarifies, "all those whom my Father hath given me out of the world" (D&C 27:5–14), multitudes of faithful Saints from the beginning of time to the end. This will be a private appearance in the sense that it will be unknown to the world. It will be a leadership meeting, a time of accounting, an accounting for priesthood stewardships. The Prophet Joseph Smith explained that Adam, the Ancient of Days, "will

call his children together and hold a council with them to prepare them for the coming of the Son of Man. He (Adam) is
the father of the human family, and presides over the spirits of
all men, and all that have had the keys must stand before him
in this grand council. . . . The Son of Man stands before him,
and there is given him [Christ] glory and dominion. Adam
delivers up his stewardship to Christ, that which was delivered
to him as holding the keys of the universe, but retains his
standing as head of the human family."[7]

President Joseph Fielding Smith explained: "This gathering of the children of Adam, where the thousands, and the
tens of thousands are assembled in the judgment, will be one
of the greatest events this troubled earth has ever seen. At this
conference, or council, all who have held keys of dispensations
will render a report of their stewardship. . . . We do not know
how long a time this will be in session, or how many sessions
will be held at this grand council. It is sufficient to know that it
is a gathering of the Priesthood of God from the beginning of
this earth down to the present, in which reports will be made
and all who have been given dispensations (talents) will
declare their keys and ministry and make report of their
stewardship. . . . This will precede the great day of destruction
of the wicked and will be the preparation for the Millennial
Reign."[8]

The Savior will appear *to the Jews on the Mount of Olives.*
It will be at the time of the Battle of Armageddon, at a time
when the Jews will find themselves with their backs against the
wall. During this period two prophets will stand before the
wicked in the streets of Jerusalem and call the people to repentance. These men, presumably members of the Council of the
Twelve Apostles or the First Presidency—holding the sealing

powers—"are to be raised up to the Jewish nation in the last days, at the time of the restoration" and will "prophesy to the Jews after they are gathered and have built the city of Jerusalem in the land of their fathers" (D&C 77:15; see also Revelation 11:4–6).[9] They will be put to death by their enemies, their bodies will lie in the streets for three and a half days, and they will then be resurrected before the assembled multitude (Revelation 11:7–12).

At about this time, the Savior will come to the rescue of the Jews (Zechariah 14:2–4). Then shall come to pass the conversion of a nation in a day, the acceptance of the Redeemer by the Jews. "And then shall the Jews look upon me and say: What are these wounds in thine hands and in thy feet? Then shall they know that I am the Lord; for I will say unto them: These wounds are the wounds with which I was wounded in the house of my friends. I am he who was lifted up. I am Jesus that was crucified. I am the Son of God. And then shall they weep because of their iniquities; then shall they lament because they persecuted their king" (D&C 45:51–53; see also Zechariah 12:10; 13:6).

Finally, and we would assume not far removed in time from his appearance on the Mount of Olives, is Christ's *coming in glory*. All will know. "Be not deceived," the Master warned in a modern revelation, "but continue in steadfastness, looking forth for the heavens to be shaken, and the earth to tremble and to reel to and fro as a drunken man, and for the valleys to be exalted, and for the mountains to be made low, and for the rough places to become smooth" (D&C 49:23; see also 133:19–22).

The righteous dead from ages past, those who qualify for the first resurrection—specifically those who died true in the faith since the time the first resurrection was initiated in the meridian of time—will come with the Savior when he returns in glory (JST 1 Thessalonians 4:13–17). Those who are of at least a terrestrial level of righteousness will continue to live as mortals after the Lord returns. During the millennial years that follow, the inhabitants of the earth will live to "the age of man"—in the words of Isaiah, the age of one hundred (Isaiah 65:20)—and will then pass through death and be changed instantly, "in the twinkling of an eye," from mortality to resurrected immortality (D&C 63:49–51; see also JST Isaiah 65:20). President Joseph Fielding Smith pointed out that "the inhabitants of the earth will have a sort of translation. They will be transferred to a condition of the terrestrial order, and so they will have power over disease and they will have power to live until they get a certain age and then they will die."[10]

Malachi prophesied that "the day cometh, that shall burn as an oven; and all the proud, yea, and all that do wickedly, shall be stubble: and the day that cometh shall burn them up, saith the Lord of hosts, that it shall leave them neither root nor branch" (Malachi 4:1; compare 2 Nephi 26:4; D&C 29:9; 64:24; 133:64; Joseph Smith–History 1:37). The second coming of Christ in glory is a day wherein "every corruptible thing, both of man, or of the beasts of the field, or of the fowls of the heavens, or of the fish of the sea, that dwells upon all the face of the earth, shall be consumed; and also that of element shall melt with fervent heat; and all things shall become new, that my knowledge and glory may dwell upon all the earth" (D&C 101:24–25; compare 133:41; 2 Peter 3:10). Joseph Fielding Smith wrote, speaking ironically: "Somebody said, 'Brother Smith, do you mean to say that it is going to be literal fire?' I said, 'Oh, no, it will not be literal fire any more than it was literal water that covered the earth in the flood.'"[11]

The revelations teach that the Savior will appear in red apparel. Red is symbolic of victory—victory over the devil, death, hell, and endless torment. It is the symbol of salvation, of being placed beyond the power of all one's enemies.[12]

Christ's red apparel will also symbolize both aspects of his ministry to fallen humanity—his mercy and his justice. Because he has trodden the winepress alone, "even the winepress of the fierceness of the wrath of Almighty God" (D&C 76:107; 88:106), he has descended below all things and mercifully taken upon him the burden of our sins. In addition, he comes in "dyed garments" as the God of justice, even he who has trampled the wicked beneath his feet (D&C 133:48–51).

The second coming in glory of Jesus Christ ushers in the Millennium. The Millennium does not begin when Christ comes to his temple in Missouri, when he appears at Adam-ondi-Ahman, or when he stands on the Mount of Olives in Jerusalem. The Millennium will not come because men and women on earth have become noble and good, because Christian charity will have spread across the globe and goodwill is the order of the day. The Millennium will not come because technological advances and medical miracles will have extended human life or because peace treaties among warring nations will have soothed injured feelings and eased political tensions for a time. The Millennium will be brought in by power, by the power of Him who is the King of kings and Lord of lords. Satan will be bound by that power, and the glory of the Millennium will be maintained by the righteousness of those who are permitted to live on the earth (1 Nephi 22:15, 26).

The early elders of the Church were instructed, "Wherefore, be of good cheer, and do not fear, for I the Lord am with you, and will stand by you; and ye shall bear record of me, even Jesus Christ, that I am the Son of the living God, that I was, that I am, and that I am to come" (D&C 68:6). This scripture says something about how we should feel about the Second Coming and about how we should approach life between now and then. As we mentioned earlier, our duty as Latter-day Saints is to so live that we enjoy the companionship, comfort, and direction of the Holy Ghost, that is, we are to live in such a manner as to fill our lamps with oil. We do not need to be truer than true, to do some marvelous and unusual thing to prepare for our Lord's return.

Those who will be caught up to meet him in the clouds of heaven, who qualify to live with him on earth during the glorious Millennium, and who then inherit exaltation in the celestial kingdom—these are they who have been true to their temple covenants, live quiet and peaceful lives, and have weaned themselves from the ways of the world. There is no mystery here, no strange or unusual requirement placed upon the Saints of the Most High; we simply need to endure faithfully to the end of our days (D&C 14:7; 50:5). There is no need to be afraid of the Second Coming, or even to fear what lies ahead. We can have hope. We can and should have rejoicing. In harmony with the soul-cry of John the Revelator, we exclaim: "Even so, come, Lord Jesus" (Revelation 22:20).

When I was a fourth grader, I was frightened when I contemplated the second coming of Christ, mostly because I didn't understand a lot of things. My views have changed as I have grown older and, I hope, a little wiser. I no longer cringe at the thought of the Second Coming. When I see and encounter the corruption and perversion that sweep our planet, when I find it harder and harder for me or my family to watch television or go to a movie without defiling ourselves, and when I ponder upon what it will be like to be taught and led and loved in person by the King of kings, I rejoice in and pray for his speedy return to earth.

NOTES

1. See *Teachings of the Prophet Joseph Smith*, 101.
2. "When Shall These Things Be?" 186.
3. *Times and Seasons*, 4:113.
4. See Bruce R. McConkie, address delivered 5 March 1971, 141–42.
5. See Bruce R. McConkie, *The Millennial Messiah*, 217, 323–27; *A New Witness for the Articles of Faith*, 521.
6. *Millennial Star*, 21:582–83.
7. *Teachings of the Prophet Joseph Smith*, 157.
8. *The Progress of Man*, 481–82; see also *The Way to Perfection*, 288–91; McConkie, *The Millennial Messiah*, 578–88.
9. See Bruce R. McConkie, *Doctrinal New Testament Commentary*, 3:509; *The Millennial Messiah*, 390.
10. *The Signs of the Times*, 42.
11. *The Signs of the Times*, 41.
12. *Teachings of the Prophet Joseph Smith*, 297, 301, 305.

17

The Victory Is Assured

Several years ago my wife and I were struggling with how best to build faith in all of our children and how to entice wandering souls back into Church activity. A caring colleague, sensing the weight of my burdens, happened into my office one day and simply asked this question: "Do you think our Heavenly Parents wander throughout the heavens in morose agony over their straying children?" Startled a bit by the question, I thought for a moment and said: "No, I don't think so. I know they feel pain, but I honestly can't picture them living in eternal misery." Then my friend responded: "Ask yourself why they do not do so and it will make a difference in your life." I didn't get much work done the rest of the day because I spent many hours pondering the question. When I arrived home that evening, I asked Shauna to sit down and reflect on the same question. She answered as I did, and then the two of us set about a prayerful quest for the next several days to understand how it is that our Eternal Father and Mother deal with their pain.

In time it began to dawn on us that the Lord knows the end from the beginning, and that, as Joseph the Prophet declared, all things—past, present, and future—are and were with Him "one eternal 'now.'"[1]

Perspective. PERSPECTIVE. That was the answer. God deals with pain through and by virtue of his infinite and perfect perspective. He not only knows what we have done and what we are doing, but he also knows what we will do in the future. If in fact, as the prophets have taught, many who are heirs to the blessings of the covenant made with Abraham, Isaac, and Jacob will either in time or eternity be reconciled to and reunited with the covenant family, then all we need to do for the time being is to seek through fasting and prayer for at least a portion of our God's perspective—his omni-loving patience, his long-suffering, his ever-open arms, and a glimpse of the big picture. Such a perspective will not only serve us well here, in the midst of our sufferings, but it will also empower our souls and fashion us into the image of our Master, who is the personification and embodiment of charity, or pure love (Moroni 7:45–48).

Knowing something about the future, the end, can help us immeasurably in dealing responsibly and productively with the present. The reason we need not succumb to cynicism or depression or despair about how awful things are now is that one day, before too very long, things will change. God is in charge. Satan may possess a huge following, and he may have great power, but God will win the battle between good and evil. As the apostle Paul declared, "Thanks be to God, [who] giveth us the victory through our Lord Jesus Christ" (1 Corinthians 15:57).

The Book of Revelation, the Apocalypse, is all about the assured victory of God and his people over the forces of evil. Even if we are uncertain as to the meanings of many of the unusual symbols in the Apocalypse, we can grasp and appreciate the overarching messages of this book of holy scripture. Some of these include:

1. Those Saints who overcome the world will receive from Christ the supernal rewards of the faithful: they will eat of the tree of life, that is, they will gain eternal life (Revelation 2:7; compare Alma 32:41); they will not be overcome by the second death (Revelation 2:11); they will come to know all things, even as God does (Revelation 2:17; D&C 130:9–11); they will gain power over many kingdoms and rule with the word of God, even as Christ, who is the bright and morning star (JST Revelation 2:26–27; 22:16); they will be adorned in white, the robes of righteousness (Revelation 3:4; 19:8); they will have the name of God written upon them, that is, they will be gods (Revelation 3:12)[2]; and they will sit with Christ on his throne, even as Christ also overcame and is set down on the throne of the Father (Revelation 3:21; compare D&C 93:20).

2. Jesus Christ, who is the Lion of the tribe of Judah, the root of David, has power to loose the seals on the record of men's dealings on this earth (Revelation 5:1–10). In other words, the Master knows the end from the beginning—he knows what was, what is, and what is to be. His is the eternal perspective, and we can trust in and rely upon his omniscient and omni-loving wisdom in orchestrating the events of our lives.

3. "Worthy is the Lamb that was slain to receive power, and riches, and wisdom, and strength, and honour, and glory, and blessing" (Revelation 5:12). Indeed, if any people in all the wide world have reason to rejoice in the Lord, it is the Latter-day Saints. When we contemplate what has been restored to earth—knowledge and power and gifts abounding—we ought

to lift our voices to heaven and exult with the Revelator, "Alleluia: for the Lord God omnipotent reigneth" (Revelation 19:6).

4. The war that began in heaven continues on earth; it will be waged until the Savior returns in glory. Many in our day are afflicted with the same poison that once afflicted Lucifer and his followers—they are "accusers of the brethren." But the faithful overcome dissidence and opposition and persecution "by the blood of the Lamb, and by the word of their testimony," for they love "not their lives unto the death" (Revelation 12:1–12).

5. Despite rising tides of wickedness, the Lord saw fit to restore the fulness of his gospel. John "saw another angel fly in the midst of heaven, having the everlasting gospel to preach unto them that dwell on the earth, and to every nation, and kindred, and tongue, and people" (Revelation 14:6). President Gordon B. Hinckley testified: "That angel has come. His name is Moroni. His is a voice speaking from the dust, bringing another witness of the living reality of the Lord Jesus Christ.

"We have not as yet carried the gospel to every nation, kindred, tongue, and people. But we have made great strides. We have gone wherever we are permitted to go. God is at the helm, and doors will be opened by His power according to His divine will. Of that I am confident. Of that I am certain."[3]

6. All people will be judged by their works out of the books that are written on earth and in heaven (Revelation 20:11–13; see also D&C 128:6–7). "He that overcometh shall inherit all things; and I will be his God, and he shall be my son" (Revelation 21:7). The faithful will become kings and priests, queens and priestesses unto God forever (Revelation 1:5–6; 5:10; 20:6).

7. Wickedness will intensify and the forces of evil will cover the globe. But the great and abominable church will eventually fall, and Satanic influences will be no more (Revelation 17–19). There will be an eventual triumph of good over evil on this earth. A day of righteousness will be ushered in at the time of our Savior's return in glory. Satan will be bound, and the work of God will go forward without distraction for a thousand years. At the end of that glorious era, the devil will be loosed for a little season, but he and his minions will be defeated by the powers of God, and a final cleansing will take place. The earth will then become the celestial kingdom (Revelation 21–22; compare D&C 88:17–20).

"Imagine that you are attending a football game," Elder Boyd K. Packer has said. "The teams seem evenly matched. One team has been trained to follow the rules; the other, to do just the opposite. They are committed to cheat and disobey every rule of sportsmanlike conduct.

"While the game ends in a tie, it is determined that it must continue until one side wins decisively.

"Soon the field is a quagmire.

"Players on both sides are being ground into the mud. The cheating of the opposing team turns to brutality.

"Players are carried off the field. Some have been injured critically; others, it is whispered, fatally. It ceases to be a game and becomes a battle.

"You become very frustrated and upset. 'Why let this go on? Neither team can win. It must be stopped.'

"Imagine that you confront the sponsor of the game and demand that he stop this useless, futile battle. You say it is senseless and without purpose. Has he no regard at all for the players?

"He calmly replies that he will not call the game. You are mistaken. There is a great purpose in it. You have not understood.

"He tells you that this is not a spectator sport—it is for the participants. It is for their sake that he permits the game to continue. Great benefit may come to them because of the challenges they face.

"He points to players sitting on the bench, suited up, eager to enter the game. 'When each one of them has been in, when each has met the day for which he has prepared so long and trained so hard, then, and only then, will I call the game.'

"Until then, it may not matter which team seems to be ahead. The present score is really not crucial. There are games within games, you know. Whatever is happening to the team, each player will have his day.

"Those players on the team that keep the rules will not be eternally disadvantaged by the appearance that their team somehow always seems to be losing.

"In the field of destiny, no team or player will be eternally disadvantaged because they keep the rules. They may be cornered or misused, even defeated for a time. But individual players on that team, regardless of what appears on the scoreboard, may already be victorious.

"Each player will have a test sufficient to his needs; how each responds is the test.

"When the game is finally over, you and they will see purpose in it all, may even express gratitude for having been on the field during the darkest part of the contest."

Then, in providing a bit of interpretation for this remarkable parable, Elder Packer added: "I do not think the Lord is quite so hopeless about what's going on in the world as we are. He could put a stop to all of it any moment. But He will not! Not until every player has a chance to meet the test for which we were preparing before the world was, before we came into mortality."[4]

It is true that perilous times lie ahead, that Gadianton bands will yet wreak havoc on this planet, that murder and immorality and deceit will extend their evil tentacles, that it will seem to us as though every man were at war with his neighbor. But there will be safety in the stakes of Zion, safety within the gospel net, safety and security to be found through standing in holy places.

While the prophetic promise is that the Lord will preserve his people (Moses 7:61), this does not necessarily mean that the righteous will always be spared the pain of loss, the agony of misrepresentation and betrayal, or even the sober reality of mortal death. The Prophet Joseph Smith explained that "it is a false idea that the Saints will escape all the judgments, whilst the wicked suffer; for all flesh is subject to suffer, and 'the righteous shall hardly escape;' still many of the Saints will escape, for the just shall live by faith; yet many of the righteous shall fall a prey to disease, to pestilence, etc., by reason of the weakness of the flesh, and yet be saved in the Kingdom of God."[5]

Elder Bruce R. McConkie thus taught: "We do not say that all of the Saints will be spared and saved from the coming day of desolation. But we do say there is no promise of safety and no promise of security except for those who love the Lord and who are seeking to do all that he commands."[6]

What I am trying to say is this: Because we know that God will win, we need not fret about the future. Because we know that the great and abominable church will crumble, we need not be discouraged as organized evil spreads its mischief. Because we know that this Church of Jesus Christ of Latter-day Saints will indeed be found in every nation and kingdom under heaven, we need not worry about this slanderous remark or that misrepresentation of our faith and way of life. The Lord lives. This is his work, and he will bring it to consummation. He will not be defeated. Nephi prophesied: "For the time soon cometh that the fulness of the wrath of God shall be poured out upon all the children of men; for he will not suffer that the wicked shall destroy the righteous. Wherefore, he will preserve the righteous by his power, even if it so be that the fulness of his wrath must come, and the righteous be preserved, even unto the destruction of their enemies by fire," meaning, the fire of the glory of Christ at the time of his second coming. "Wherefore," Nephi stated, "the righteous need not fear; for thus saith the prophet, they shall be saved, even if it so be as by fire" (1 Nephi 22:16–17).

Brigham Young University professor Todd A. Britsch told a delightful story that illustrates the power and peace that come of knowing that the victory is assured. "A few years ago," he said, "before the time that all BYU games were televised live, I landed at the Salt Lake airport just as a BYU 'away' game was concluding. I rushed around the terminal until I finally found someone who could assure me that we had won, although by a very close score. That evening, after returning to Provo, I went downstairs to watch the replay of the game on KBYU. My demeanor was amazingly serene. When we fumbled or had a pass intercepted, I hardly reacted. My wife could even let our children get around me. Usually I feel obligated to help my brethren in striped shirts by pointing out their errors in judgment. Because my seats are on row 25, such correction often requires a rather high decibel level. This loudness has carried over to watching football on television. But on that day I remained absolutely calm, even when I had the benefit of instant replay to verify my claim that their defensive back clearly arrived early and that the ground had obviously caused our running back to lose the ball. I was a veritable model of football decorum, never becoming unduly upset or ill behaved.

"The cause of my improved behavior was obvious: I already knew the outcome of the game—BYU would win. It is amazing how that knowledge changes things: cornerbacks can get beat, running backs can fumble, linebackers can miss tackles, offensive guards can blow blocking assignments, and other things can go wrong. But when we know the final score, such things can be endured and sometimes even ignored.

"We also know the final score for the history of this world and for the life of the righteous. The Lord and his people will triumph. It is true that the sorrows of this world and the strength of Satan's forces will win a number of the skirmishes. . . . Satan and his followers, as well as the natural circumstances of mortal life, will inflict many bruises and win many battles. But God, who knows the end from the beginning, has promised that those who serve him will receive the fullness of his blessings. When we realize that righteous living puts us on the winning side, we can learn to trust him during trying times."[7]

The Savior and his anointed servants have invited you and me to live and act today as the victors—with quiet confidence, with assurance, and with an optimism born not of arrogance but of trust in and reliance upon Him who has all power. We can face the traumas of the present because we know

something about what lies ahead. We proceed confidently in
the war against evil because of our confidence in the Captain
of our souls.

NOTES

1. *Teachings of the Prophet Joseph Smith*, 220.

2. See Orson Pratt, *Journal of Discourses*, 14:242–43.

3. Conference Report, October 1995, 93.

4. Conference Report, October 1983, 21–22.

5. *Teachings of the Prophet Joseph Smith*, 162.

6. Conference Report, April 1979, 133.

7. "Trusting God When Things Go Wrong," 30.

Epilogue

Beauty for Ashes

———— ❧ ❧ ————

Some seven hundred years before the birth of Jesus of Nazareth, Isaiah uttered prophetic words that would find their fulfillment largely in the mortal ministry of the Anointed One: "The Spirit of the Lord God is upon me; because the Lord hath anointed me to preach good tidings unto the meek; he hath sent me *to bind up the broken-hearted, to proclaim liberty to the captives, and the opening of the prison to them that are bound*; to proclaim the acceptable year of the Lord, . . . *to comfort all that mourn.*" Now note the poignant passage that follows: "To appoint unto them that mourn in Zion, *to give unto them beauty for ashes, the oil of joy for mourning,* the garment of praise for the spirit of heaviness" (Isaiah 61:1–3; emphasis added; compare Luke 4:18–19).

Jesus Christ came to bring beauty for ashes—to replace distress with comfort, worry with peace, turmoil with rest. The Good Shepherd came to earth on a "search and rescue mission"—to identify and gather in those who have strayed, to welcome the wanderer back home, to adorn the tattered son or daughter of God with a robe and a ring, to kill the fatted calf in celebration. Our Precious Savior condescended—left his throne divine—to come down and be with his people, the sheep of his fold. He came to right all the terrible wrongs of this life, to fix the unfixable, to repair the irreparable. He came to heal us by his tender touch, to still the storms of our startled hearts. Again, he came to replace ashes with beauty.

Because things do not always turn out as we had expected, because today was not the day we bargained for, "every one of us," Elder Jeffrey R. Holland has pointed out, "has times when we need to know things will get better. The Book of Mormon speaks of this as 'hope for a better world' (Ether 12:4). For emotional health and spiritual stamina, everyone needs to be able to look forward to some respite, to do something pleasant and renewing and hopeful, whether that blessing be near at hand or still some distance ahead. . . .

"My declaration is that this is precisely what the gospel of Jesus Christ offers us, especially in times of need. There *is* help. There *is* happiness. There really *is* light at the end of the tunnel. It is the Light of the World. . . . I say: Hold on. Keep trying. God loves you. Things will improve. Christ comes to you in his 'more excellent ministry' with a future of 'better promises.'"[1]

Each one of us needs to know—needs the conviction, deep down in our souls—that our Master is not an absentee Landlord, not a distant Deity. He is "touched with the feeling of our infirmities" (Hebrews 4:15), knows from firsthand experience all about our pains, our afflictions, our temptations (Alma 7:11–12), and thereby understands "the weakness of man and how to succor them who are tempted" (D&C 62:1). He has not, as the deists believed centuries ago, wound up the world clock and left it to run on its own. Rather, he is intimately involved in saving and succoring—literally, running to help—those who call upon him and learn to trust in his mighty arm. Indeed, our God's infinity does not preclude either his immediacy or his intimacy. As Enoch the seer learned, when we need God, when we reach out to him, he is there, his bosom is there; he is just and merciful and kind forever (Moses 7:30).

Many in the free world were tempted at the time of the great tragedy on 11 September 2001 to cry out: Where is God? Where was he when we needed him? Could he not have prevented this heinous deed? As we discussed in chapter 2, our God, though an exalted Man of Holiness, is also all-powerful, has all knowledge, and is, by the power of his Spirit, everywhere present. He could, if he chose to do so, prevent every tragedy and block every trauma. But he will not do so, for such would thwart the great plan of happiness by impinging upon the moral agency of both the wicked and the righteous.

One person has responded to questions about God's presence and involvement in our world as follows: "I know where my God was the morning of September 11, 2001. He was very busy. First of all, he was trying to discourage anyone from taking this flight. Those four flights together [could have] held over 1000 passengers, [but] there were only 266 aboard. He was on four commercial flights giving terrified passengers the ability to stay calm. Not one of the family members who was called by a loved one on one of the hijacked planes said that passengers were screaming in the background. On one of the flights he was giving strength to passengers to try to overtake the hijackers. He was busy trying to create obstacles for employees at the World Trade Center [so they wouldn't be at work]. After all, only around 20,000 were at the towers when the first jet hit. Since the buildings hold over 50,000 workers, this was a miracle in itself. How many of the people who were employed at the World Trade Center told the media that they were late for work or they had traffic delays? He [God] was holding up two 110-story buildings so that [four-fifths] of the workers could get out."[2]

Returning to Isaiah's prophecy with which we began this chapter, we are reminded that the Lord promises to give "the oil of joy for mourning, the garment of praise for the spirit of heaviness" (Isaiah 61:3). As we open ourselves to his redeeming and enabling power, Jesus pours oil on the troubled waters of our lives, and clothes us in the quiet assurance of his sanctifying praise. When we have learned to lean on the Lord and rely on his goodness and his approval, then what the world thinks of us comes to matter precious little. When the fickle plaudits of the worldly wise no longer entice us, then we are buoyed up by the sweet peace that signals divine approval. "I receive not honour from men" (John 5:41), Jesus declared. And so it is with those who confess him as Lord and Master. We cry out: "Hear, O Lord, and have mercy upon me: Lord, be thou my helper. Thou hast turned for me my mourning into dancing: thou hast put off my sackcloth, and girded me with gladness" (Psalm 30:10–11).

During my darkest hours—during times of extreme stress and distress or days of worry and deep anxiety—comfort and perspective have come through singing or reflecting upon the words of sacred music. For example:

> *Be still, my soul: The Lord is on thy side;*
> *With patience bear thy cross of grief or pain.*
> *Leave to thy God to order and provide;*
> *In ev'ry change he faithful will remain.*
> *Be still, my soul: Thy best, thy heav'nly Friend*
> *Thru thorny ways leads to a joyful end.*

Be still, my soul: Thy God doth undertake
To guide the future as he has the past.
Thy hope, thy confidence let nothing shake;
All now mysterious shall be bright at last.
Be still, my soul: The waves and winds still know
His voice who ruled them while he dwelt below.

Be still, my soul: The hour is hast'ning on
When we shall be forever with the Lord,
When disappointment, grief, and fear are gone,
Sorrow forgot, love's purest joys restored.
Be still, my soul: When change and tears are past,
All safe and blessed we shall meet at last.[3]

As I have sought to point out more than once in this work, we need not be free from turmoil or sorrow in order to be at rest in today's world. Like Nephi, we need not know the meaning of all things to know that the Savior loves us (1 Nephi 11:17) and that he can strengthen us to bear heavy burdens with relative ease. Let us be reminded that "whatever Jesus lays his hands upon lives. If Jesus lays his hands upon a marriage, it lives. If he is allowed to lay his hands on the family, it lives."[4]

The Lord is not slack in keeping his promises to his chosen people: he will give "beauty for ashes, the oil of joy for mourning, the garment of praise for the spirit of heaviness." He will welcome his faithful Saints into "the rest of the Lord" (Moroni 7:3), not only in the sense of granting them eternal life in the world to come, but also in bestowing upon them the peace which is the harbinger of eternal life (D&C 59:23), the peace in this life that passes all understanding (Philippians 4:7). God may not always remove us from the burdensome and toilsome circumstances in which we find ourselves, but he will empower us to deal responsibly with and even change the circumstances.

The rest of the Lord is "a settled conviction of the truth in the minds of men." "To my mind," President Joseph F. Smith observed, entering into the rest of the Lord "means entering into the knowledge and love of God, having faith in his purpose and in his plan." This is a condition the world as a whole cannot comprehend, for it is "rest from doubt, from fear, from apprehension of danger, rest from the religious turmoil of the world."[5] Mormon thus spoke of "the peaceable followers of Christ [who] have obtained a sufficient hope by which ye can enter into the rest of the Lord, from this time henceforth until ye shall rest with him in heaven" (Moroni 7:3).

In speaking of the horror and tragedy of the events of 11 September 2001, President Gordon B. Hinckley stated: "Our hearts are deeply touched. . . . This has been a tragic, solemn and dark day. We have been reminded that evil is still rampant in the world. Its insidious and dastardly hand has struck again in a most reprehensible manner." Now note the calming reassurance from a prophet of God: "But dark as is this hour, there is shining through the heavy overcast of fear and anger the solemn and wonderful image of the Son of God, the Savior of the world, the Prince of Peace, the exemplar of universal love, and it is to Him that we look in these circumstances. It was He who gave His life that all might enjoy eternal life. May the peace of Christ rest upon us and give us comfort and reassurance."[6]

Life is good. I love life. Like you, I have experienced pain and fear and frustration and anguish of soul. Like you, I have had those dark moments when I have asked, Why? Why am I being asked to pass through this miserable and unsettling situation, especially when we have tried so hard to do what's right? And so I know something about the sufferings and struggles that accompany life in this second estate. But there are so many wonderful blessings to be gained and lasting lessons to be learned through passing through the refiner's fire, particularly at this exciting time in earth's history. There is so much to look forward to.

"And one of the elders answered, saying unto me, What are these [people who] are arrayed in white robes? and whence came they? And I said unto him, Sir, thou knowest. And he said to me, These are they which came out of great tribulation, and have washed their robes, and made them white in the blood of the Lamb. Therefore are they before the throne of God, and serve him day and night in his temple: and he that sitteth on the throne shall dwell among them. They shall hunger no more, neither thirst any more; neither shall the sun light on them, nor any heat. For the Lamb which is in the midst of the throne shall feed them, and shall lead them unto living fountains of waters: and God shall wipe away all tears from their eyes" (Revelation 7:13–17).

I echo the counsel of the prophets of God, ancient and modern, that we need not fear, we need not surrender to despair or doom or gloom. God is in his heavens. He knows us, one and all, and he knows of our pains and our possibilities. Jesus Christ our Deliverer lives, is directing his Church and kingdom through living prophets and apostles, and offers to bear our burdens and liberate our souls from the galling yoke of sin and the fetters of a fading world. I rejoice in the privilege it is to be a part of the dispensation of the fulness of times, to be a participant in the winding-up scenes. And I look forward, more than I can say, to the return in glory of our Lord and Savior and to life with him and the faithful Saints of all ages.

NOTES

1. Conference Report, October 1999, 45.
2. Author unknown.
3. Katharina von Schlegel, "Be Still, My Soul," in *Hymns of The Church of Jesus Christ of Latter-day Saints*, no. 124.
4. Howard W. Hunter, Conference Report, October 1979, 93.
5. *Gospel Doctrine*, 58, 126.
6. Address, 11 September 2001, Salt Lake Tabernacle.

BIBLIOGRAPHY

Ballard, M. Russell. "When Shall These Things Be?" *1995–96 BYU Speeches of the Year*. Provo: BYU Publications, 1996.

Benson, Ezra Taft. *A Witness and a Warning*. Salt Lake City: Deseret Book Co., 1988.

Bonhoeffer, Dietrich. *The Cost of Discipleship*. New York: Macmillan, 1963.

Britsch, Todd A. "Trusting God When Things Go Wrong." *1997–98 BYU Speeches of the Year*. Provo: BYU Publications, 1998.

Conference Report. Salt Lake City: The Church of Jesus Christ of Latter-day Saints, April 1942; April 1943; April 1968; October 1972; October 1973; October 1974; April 1978; April 1979; October 1979; October 1983; April 1985; October 1985; October 1988; October 1989; October 1992; October 1994; April 1995; October 1995; October 1997; April 1999; October 1999; April 2001.

Faust, James E. *Finding Light in a Dark World*. Salt Lake City: Deseret Book Co., 1995.

Frankl, Victor. *Man's Search for Meaning*. New York: Washington Square Press, 1985.

Hafen, Bruce C., and Marie K. Hafen. *The Belonging Heart*. Salt Lake City: Deseret Book Co., 1994.

Hinckley, Gordon B. Address to The National Association of Insurance and Financial Underwriters, 11 September 2001, Salt Lake Tabernacle.

———. *Teachings of Gordon B. Hinckley*. Salt Lake City: Deseret Book Co., 1997.

Holland, Jeffrey R. *Christ and the New Covenant*. Salt Lake City: Deseret Book Co., 1997.

Hymns of The Church of Jesus Christ of Latter-day Saints. Salt Lake City: The Church of Jesus Christ of Latter-day Saints, 1985.

Journal of Discourses. 26 vols. Liverpool: F. D. Richards & Sons, 1854–86.

Kimball, Spencer W. *Faith Precedes the Miracle*. Salt Lake City: Deseret Book Co., 1974.

Latter-day Saints' Messenger and Advocate. Kirtland, Ohio: The Church of Jesus Christ of Latter-day Saints, 1834–35.

Lee, Harold B. "Cram for Life's Final Examination." *BYU Speeches of the Year*. Provo: BYU Publications, 5 January 1954.

———. LDS Student Association fireside, Utah State University, 10 October 1971 (unofficial transcript).

———. *Stand Ye in Holy Places*. Salt Lake City: Deseret Book Co., 1974.

———. *Ye Are the Light of the World*. Salt Lake City: Deseret Book Co., 1974.

Lewis, C. S. *Letters to Malcolm: Chiefly on Prayer*. New York: Harcourt, 1992.

———. *Mere Christianity*. New York: Touchstone Books, 1996.

———. *The Problem of Pain*. New York: Touchstone Books, 1996.

Maxwell, Neal A. *Things As They Really Are*. Salt Lake City: Deseret Book Co., 1978.

McConkie, Bruce R. Address delivered 5 March 1971 to returned Korean missionaries, Provo, Utah. In Spencer J. Palmer. *The Expanding Church*. Salt Lake City: Deseret Book Co., 1978.

———. *Doctrinal New Testament Commentary*. 3 vols. Salt Lake City: Bookcraft, 1965–73.

———. *Doctrines of the Restoration*. Edited by Mark L. McConkie. Salt Lake City: Bookcraft, 1989.

———. *The Millennial Messiah*. Salt Lake City: Deseret Book Co., 1982.

———. *A New Witness for the Articles of Faith*. Salt Lake City: Deseret Book Co., 1985.

McKay, David O. *Gospel Ideals*. Salt Lake City: Improvement Era, 1953.

Messages of the First Presidency. 6 vols. Compiled by James R. Clark. Salt Lake City: Bookcraft, 1965–75.

Millennial Star. Liverpool: The Church of Jesus Christ of Latter-day Saints, 1840–1970.

Muggeridge, Malcolm. *Jesus: The Man Who Lives*. New York: Harper & Row, 1975.

Packer, Boyd K. "Follow the Brethren," *1965 Brigham Young University Speeches of the Year*. Provo: BYU Publications, 1965.

———. *The Holy Temple*. Salt Lake City: Bookcraft, 1980.

————. "The Play and the Plan," Church Educational System Fireside, 7 May 1995, satellite broadcast from Kirkland, Washington.

————. *Teach Ye Diligently.* Salt Lake City: Deseret Book Co., 1975.

————. *That All May Be Edified.* Salt Lake City: Bookcraft, 1982.

————. *The Things of the Soul.* Salt Lake City: Bookcraft, 1996.

Plantinga, Cornelius. *Not the Way It's Supposed to Be: A Breviary of Sin.* Grand Rapids, Michigan: William B. Eerdmans Publishing Co., 1995.

Romney, Marion G. "A Glorious Promise." *Ensign,* January 1981.

————. *Learning for the Eternities.* Salt Lake City: Deseret Book Co., 1977.

Shoemaker, Donald P. "Why Your Neighbor Joined the Mormon Church." *Christianity Today,* 11 October 1974.

Smith, Joseph, Jr. *Lectures on Faith.* Salt Lake City: Deseret Book Co., 1985.

————. *The Personal Writings of Joseph Smith.* Edited by Dean C. Jessee. Salt Lake City: Deseret Book Co., 1984.

————. *Teachings of the Prophet Joseph Smith.* Selected by Joseph Fielding Smith. Salt Lake City: Deseret Book Co., 1976.

Smith, Joseph F. *Gospel Doctrine.* Salt Lake City: Deseret Book Co., 1971.

————. Letter to Hyrum M. Smith, 18 May 1896. In *From Prophet to Son: Advice of Joseph F. Smith to His Missionary Sons.* Compiled by Hyrum M. Smith III and Scott G. Kenney. Salt Lake City: Deseret Book Co., 1981.

Smith, Joseph Fielding. *Doctrines of Salvation.* 3 vols. Compiled by Bruce R. McConkie. Salt Lake City: Bookcraft, 1954–56.

————. *The Progress of Man.* Salt Lake City: Deseret Book Co., 1964.

————. *The Signs of the Times.* Salt Lake City: Deseret Book Co., 1952.

————. *The Way to Perfection.* Salt Lake City: Deseret Book Co., 1970.

Stanley, Charles. *The Blessings of Brokenness.* Grand Rapids, Michigan: Zondervan, 1997.

Swinburne, Richard. *Is There a God?* New York: Oxford University Press, 1996.

Times and Seasons. 6 vols. Nauvoo, Illinois: The Church of Jesus Christ of Latter-day Saints, 1839–46.

Woodruff, Wilford. *Leaves from My Journal.* Salt Lake City: Juvenile Instructor Office, 1881.

INDEX